# THE CARPET GARDEN

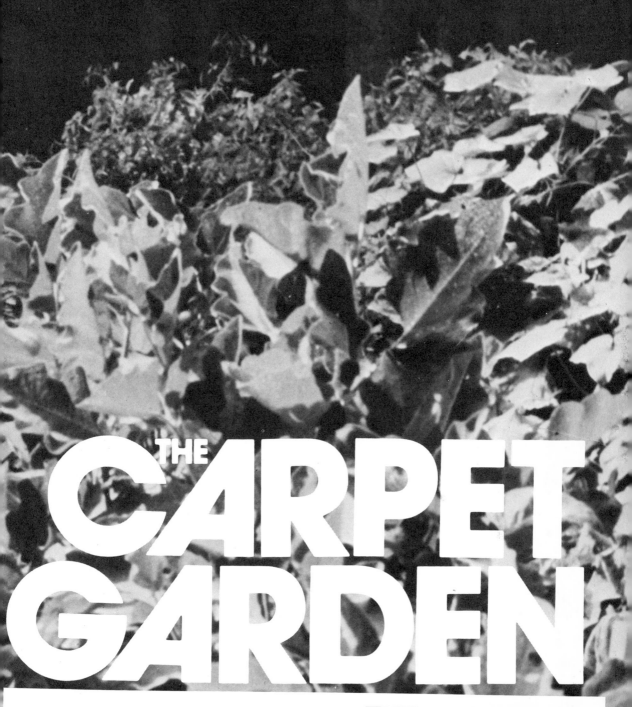

# THE CARPET GARDEN

## THE ANSWER TO NO-WORK VEGETABLE GARDENING FOR LESS THAN $5 PER SUMMER

## By Renée and Steve Rockmore

THOMAS Y. CROWELL COMPANY
New York/Established 1834

Photography by Bob Witt and Steve Rockmore
Drawings, jacket and book design by Steve Rockmore

FIRST EDITION

**Library of Congress Cataloging in Publication Data**

Rockmore, Renée.
  The carpet garden.

  Includes index.
  1.  Vegetable gardening.  2.  Mulching.
3.  Carpets.  I.  Rockmore, Steve, joint author.
II.  Title.
SB321.R59  1978     635′.0973     77-27434
ISBN 0-690-01679-4
ISBN 0-690-01747-2 pbk.

78 79 80 81 82 10 9 8 7 6 5 4 3 2 1

To Thomas E. Carroll who knows

# CONTENTS

# The No-Work Garden for Less Than $5 Per Summer

Have you ever yearned for a work-free garden? One that is not only prolific and attractive, but is absolutely weedless?

Have you ever wished you could have a garden that doesn't need watering? Or one that allows you to plant your vegetables earlier in the year?

Have you ever dreamed of having a garden that produces the same quantity of vegetables as one four times its size? Or of owning a garden that actually rejects bugs?

And have you ever thought you could have all this convenience and productivity for an average carpet investment of less than $5 per summer?

This book is all about just such a garden—and, believe it or not, this garden actually exists. In fact, it has been flourishing for five summers on our property in upstate New York.

We call this revolutionary method of raising vegetables *Carpet Gardening* and consider it to be the ultimate in modern vegetable raising. It is wonderfully successful gardening at a fantastically economical cost, and it requires only 10 percent of the work that traditional gardens demand. And its yield is four times that of other gardens.

Yes, Carpet Gardening is truly low cost. In fact, we feel this extraordinary new method of mulching has to be the least expensive of all known mulches. While it may at first appear to be an extravagant method of controlling weeds in the garden, the lifespan of the carpeting and the many other advantages that come with its use make it the most practical mulching material ever conceived. The carpeting itself should last twenty years at the very least, based on the results of exhaustive testing, and the cost to you averages out to only $5 per summer for a large 15' $\times$ 24' carpet garden. For a

9

thorough discussion of the economics of the carpeting, see pages 21–23 in Chapter One.

We can state with absolute confidence that a Carpet Garden means no weeding, no cultivating, no spraying, no dusting, almost no watering—and no worrying. Whether you are a veteran gardener or one of the twenty million new gardeners each year, you owe it to yourself to have a no-work garden that will pay off in both dollars and sheer pleasure.

Why subject yourself to the drudgery of weeding, cultivating, bug spraying, and all the other demands that come with traditional gardens? Why complicate the joy of raising vegetables with an overwhelming dedication to fertilizers and an enslavement to plant protection? Well, we are pleased to tell you that all that drudgery, contrary to popular belief, does *not* "come with the territory." You can have a lovely, wonderfully productive garden with only a minimal amount of effort and expense, a garden that is grown as it should be—without chemical sprays, weeds, and endless tending.

You say that the last time you saw something like that was in the Garden of Eden? Well, take heart because you can have this garden, right in your own backyard, for you to admire and harvest, without backbreaking labor.

In all fairness, we realize there are those of you who find the most difficult of gardening chores relaxing and pleasurable and who prefer to cultivate a conventional garden. You know who you are and this book is not for you. This book *is* for all the rest of us who love gardens but don't have the time to spend every weekend working (and we mean *working*) in them. This book is for those of us who love garden-fresh vegetables and get satisfaction from watching them grow, yet who also love having the free time to enjoy the fruits—or shall we say the vegetables—of our labors.

We can promise you that with the Carpet Garden method the only chores you'll have are the three most pleasurable tasks of gardening: planning, planting, and harvesting.

# Introduction

The first year that we purchased carpeting for our garden, our friends and neighbors tried to talk us out of the idea. They felt we would be wasting a perfectly good carpet by putting it in the dirt and trying to make a garden out of it. They went on to insist that it was never intended to be placed directly on the ground, and that it would surely destroy anything we planted.

Some doomsayers believed it would provide a happy home for garden varmints, who would be able to remain snug and safe from enemies. The skeptics went on to predict that moles, mice, and groundhogs—even chipmunks—would line up, waiting for us to put it down.

Others were firmly convinced that we would be guaranteeing problems such as "root rot" and that our onions would soon turn to slime.

We did, in short, hear every conceivable discouraging word that the prophets of doom could summon—all the reasons why the Carpet Garden would fail. *However,* all we know is that it worked fantastically well that first summer. In fact, after five summers of staggering success, we are proud to say that almost all of our non-believing neighbors have carpeted gardens today.

But we don't want to get ahead of ourselves. We want you to know that before our discovery of the carpet method of gardening we made many attempts at gardening, employing more traditional methods—methods which, although highly problematical and subject to the vagaries of weather, physical stamina of the gardener, pestilence, and divine providence, were the only options.

We can easily recall the sight of those green grapes that were supposed to be tomatoes, the carrots that took on the shape of stubby pencils, and the lettuce that was so riddled with grub holes that it wouldn't sway in even a hurricane-force wind.

Back then, too, we spent many weekends cursing the weeds that flourished in the garden and the rabbits that feasted on the first new growth. And, although we sprayed and dusted, nothing that grew even vaguely resembled the pictures on the seed packages.

We were determined to raise our own vegetables, so we turned to mulch gardening the next year. We tilled, fertilized, and marked on the calendar certain dates taken from the collection of dog-eared gardening pages we had been carefully saving over the years.

We made what we hoped would be a happy home for two praying mantises, whom we were counting on to be our garden's guardians, and spread costly bales of hay mulch far and wide. Then, confident that we had done our part, we left the second stage to Mother Nature. However, Mother Nature had apparently been liberated that second summer, as she didn't lift a finger to help in her share of the work.

We had been warned that this method of mulch gardening would not be 100 percent effective against weeds unless we mulched very, very deeply. And so we obeyed, and what a mess there was to clean up in the fall! Not only did we have to contend with removing the stones that kept the mulch in place (we get some pretty strong gusts of wind in our neck of the woods), but we had a real problem getting rid of the mulch which, during the course of the summer, had become infested with insects and field mice.

Our third failure in vegetable gardening came with our trial of the black-plastic technique. This method of mulch gardening, we were promised, was the answer to the no-weed garden and was very popular in our area of upstate New York.

We have to admit that at first the results were phenomenal. However, as we progressed toward midsummer, it became evident that our plants were suffering from a lack of water. This, of course, was due to the fact that even with perforations the plastic did not allow adequate rainfall to reach the roots of the plants. Instead, it caused the water to lie in puddles on the surface, playing host to an army of mosquitoes and other insects.

In trying all these methods, our goal was, quite simply, to have a vegetable garden that would provide us with fresh vegetables throughout the summer months. We were intent on achieving this goal but, at the same time, wanted to dispense with some of the time-consuming and distasteful chores.

Neither of us found any pleasure in weeding, spraying, dusting—in laboring in the garden. We both could easily think of more gratifying chores to be performed about the house.

In all of these first attempts, we had taken the advice of friends and neighbors and, although we enjoyed partial success, the end results hardly seemed worth the effort. The produce from these first gardens was small and, for the most part, unattractive. The hard work, the many weekends of weeding, watering, and worrying brought only disappointment. No matter what method we used, we always were very careful to prepare the soil properly, so we knew that was not the problem, yet we failed anyway, every time. We soon began to feel that the whole business of gardening was better left to the professionals who, somehow, held the secret to those giant tomatoes, the super zucchini, and the perfect peppers that always looked as if they had just taken all the prizes at the county fair.

It wasn't until the fourth summer that we found the solution to successful gardening—an answer so perfect, so amazing that now, *even we* can have a vegetable garden that far surpasses the Green Thumb Vegetable Market. Now we can mix our drinks and relax in the shade of a large tree and watch the most spectacular of all gardens blossom before our eyes.

We sent that pair of praying mantises back to the supplier. We retired all the old garden tools, rolled up the water hose, threw away the weed puller, shelved the poison sprays, and told the bugs to bug off.

We've learned the secret of successful gardening. We no longer worry about weeding during those hot summer days or forgetting to water. In fact, with our new method of gardening, we no longer dust, spray, spade, water, or weed.

All we do now is plant and harvest. The quantity and the quality of the harvest are so great that we have plenty left over to give our friends and neighbors who so kindly offered the advice that ruined our lives for three full summers.

# CHAPTER 1

# The Advantages of the Carpet Garden

The advantages of the Carpet Garden are many, as you will see from this discussion of its remarkable qualities.

## NO WEEDING

Basically, the only answer to a weed-free garden is to prevent the sunlight from reaching the soil areas surrounding your plants. Such a practice is called mulching.

*Anything* that can be used to cover the soil without injuring the plants or damaging the soil can be considered mulch. Hay, leaves, mulching paper, newspaper, pine needles, grass clippings, ground corncobs, sawdust, wood chips, wood shavings, straws (such as wheat, rye, oat, and barley), salt or natural marsh hay, sugar cane, peat moss, and even seaweed have been used to keep the relentless weeds from entering the garden.

Although all of these mulches do, to a certain degree, prevent sunlight from reaching the soil and considerably reduce weed growth in the garden, they all have two things in common: they're all temporary and basically unattractive. And, as we have said, they all tend to act as havens for various pesky little beasts—many varieties of insects as well as field mice. No one in his right mind wants to run a hotel for mice, as we are sure you agree. And, as we also explained in our introduction, once the mulch has become infested it is an incredible bother to clean up—if you can figure out where to dump the mess.

In choosing the best possible mulch for your garden, you must consider cost, lifespan, availability, ease of handling, and general appearance. It is for all of these reasons that we chose to use indoor/

17

outdoor carpeting for our garden.

Of all the mulches that we tried on our garden in the Catskill region of New York State, probably the one which came closest to giving us a no-work garden was black polyethylene. While the black plastic outlasts most other coverings, it cannot be expected to survive more than four or five years. It tears easily and requires stones, wire mesh, or weights of some kind to keep it in place. Black plastic also does not allow rainfall to penetrate the surface and, because most vegetables require upward of two inches of rain per week, use of the plastic can and will stunt the growth of many plants. To compensate for this impenetrability, a great many holes must be made in the plastic. Another disadvantage is the shiny, jet-black color. Dark colors absorb light far more than light tones and, during the hottest part of the summer, you can be sure that the soil beneath the plastic will become excessively dry, requiring constant watering.

Indoor/outdoor carpeting used as mulch possesses none of these undesirable characteristics. The carpet can take incredible abuse, will last as long as twenty years, does not tear easily, does not contaminate the soil, is porous and consequently allows natural rainfall to penetrate its surface, is heavy enough to stay put with no added weights, and comes in a variety of colors to make the most of your particular climate region, as explained below.

## NO WATERING

Most garden crops, whether the leaf, root, or fruit of a plant, consist principally of water. Abundant, vigorous crops will result if the plants are *never* allowed to suffer from a lack of water.

As soon as the surface soil on any garden becomes dry, it is time to water. However, if the surface is not allowed to dry out, the amount of water you need to add can be held to a minimum.

Because indoor/outdoor carpeting is basically porous, rainfall is able to penetrate to the roots of the plants where it is needed. The great advantage of using such carpeting, however, is its wonderful ability to retain this precious moisture. It is nothing short of life-saving during dry spells because it allows only small amounts of water to evaporate, keeping the soil below moist.

The ability of the carpet to perform in such a way is due to its thickness as well as to the particular shade you choose. The condition of the soil also affects moisture retention, discussed on page 34.

The thickness of the carpet insulates the surface soil and does not allow it to heat up rapidly. Consequently, the moisture content in the soil beneath the surface is less apt to change drastically from day to day, thereby ensuring a relatively consistent climate.

18

The color of the carpet you choose for your garden can greatly assist in keeping moisture in the soil. Because dark colors tend to absorb light and heat, and light colors to reflect them, it becomes obvious how the choice of color will affect the temperature and thus the moisture content of the soil. For our climate in upstate New York, we shy away from the darkest colors, which we fear will heat the garden too much in July and August and dry out the soil. Yet light colors tend to keep the soil a bit too cool when, in early spring, it should be the intention to warm it up. A happy compromise is to choose a medium tone, such as our medium blue-green. But indoor/outdoor carpeting comes in a wide variety of colors. There are hues like mustard, sea green, wine, gold, and barn red—not to mention the many other colors that should be appearing any day now, in response to the popularity of our Carpet Gardening system (like tomato red, bean yellow, zucchini green, and endive white). We recommend that you take your region's climate into consideration— its rainfall, sunlight, and temperature range—before selecting your color.

The best way to tell if the plants in the garden are getting sufficient water is to occasionally lift the edge of the carpet and feel the soil. If the soil is dry, give the carpet a soaking. We also pay attention to the cucumbers. Have you ever noticed a cucumber which is small at the stem end and suddenly swells out to normal size, or one that starts off nobly only to be squeezed down to something that looks much like a pencil, or possibly a specimen which swells and shrinks and swells again? Well, if this begins to happen, you couldn't ask for a better signal to get out the hose. This will be a rare event.

## EARLIER PLANTING

The heat-absorbing and heat-retaining properties of indoor/outdoor carpeting will warm the soil beneath the carpet in the early spring. This, of course, allows us to plant earlier than most and, consequently, we invariably beat our neighbors to the harvest each and every year.

Not only do we enjoy many fresh vegetables during midsummer but this advantage makes double cropping possible during the planting season.

The time for planting is very important—from the standpoint of having vigorous, productive plants and for simply ensuring their survival. For example, eggplants that are set in the Carpet Garden before the ground is warm and before daily temperatures are high simply will not grow. Conversely, peas that are planted too late in the spring to mature before the intense summer heat prevails will not

19

be productive. So planting must be planned to coincide with each vegetable's temperature requirements.

Extremely cold-hardy plants which can be planted in early spring include radishes, lettuce, chard, parsnips, beets, carrots, and onions. Those vegetables which should be planted in midspring include beans, squash, New Zealand spinach (it's great!), and tomatoes. The really heat-hardy vegetables that go to town in hot weather are lima beans, eggplants, peppers, and cucumbers. The cold-fighters that thrive in the fall include kale, beets, turnips, late cabbage, and lettuce.

While you can get a head start, a Carpet Garden won't make it possible for you to plant as soon as the snow melts. Some vegetables are frost tender; some are hardy; some like it cool and some like it hot. To be sure you are planting the right vegetables at the right time, check the planting guide on pages 112–117.

## A LONGER HARVEST SEASON

Last fall, when the old killer frost came rolling in, it seemed like only a day or two before almost all of the gardens in our area had begun to wilt and show signs of weariness.

Strangely enough, although the frost appeared on our garden, it was only noticeable at the very tops of the tallest plants, such as the peppers and tomatoes, and those which hung on the fence. Aside from these, a great many low-lying, smaller plants, such as cherry tomatoes, onions, lettuce, chard, zucchini, herbs, and scallions were doing better than ever.

What this suggested to us was that the Carpet Garden had managed to keep the soil warm during this first frost and that those plants which grew short or hung low enough managed to pull through.

It was almost four weeks later that a second, more severe frost came sweeping down, and we knew we didn't have a chance. However, it didn't really matter this time, because we had harvested almost all the remaining vegetables.

## SPACE SAVING AND FOUR TIMES
## AS GREAT PRODUCTIVITY

One of the most important advantages of Carpet Gardening is that it uses less space than other types of gardens. By using the indoor/outdoor carpet method, you will be able to plant your garden in one-quarter of the space required in traditional types of gardens.

The reason for this is that traditional gardens require a minimum of 18 inches between rows to allow for cultivation. Using the carpet method, however, you will be able to plant as many as four rows of vegetables within this space because weeding and cultivation will no longer be necessary. This closer spacing still allows proper plant nourishment. The before and after plans of our garden on page 23 clearly demonstrate how a Carpet Garden can provide a harvest equal to traditional gardens measuring four times its size. For detailed information on plant spacing in the Carpet Garden, see pages 43–44 in Chapter Four.

The best illustration of the Carpet Garden's four-times-as-great productivity is provided by comparing the test results of experiments performed by the Illinois Department of Horticulture with our results. In 1975, the Department of Horticulture initiated gardens in various parts of Illinois as a service to the increasing number of people who were attempting to grow some of their own food.

A small garden measuring 840 square feet (12 by 70 feet) was located on the Pharmacognosy and Horticulture Field Station at Downers Grove, Illinois. The Downers Grove garden provided an edible yield worth $145. Investment in seeds and transplants amounted to $11.50.

During this same summer, we had installed a Carpet Garden measuring 180 square feet (10 by 18 feet) on our property in Kingston, New York. The Carpet Garden produced an edible yield worth $163. Investment in seeds and transplants amounted to $12.15.

The result was, of course, that the Carpet Garden actually produced a greater edible yield in less than one-quarter of the space used at the Downers Grove experiment.

Identical methods of planting were used in both the Carpet Garden and the Downers Grove garden of the Department of Horticulture. Maximum use of space was achieved by double cropping or planting a second crop after an early-maturing species was harvested. (For those of you who might wish to practice double cropping, we have prepared a table giving vegetable growth times. You will find this table in the appendix of this book.)

We attribute this advantage in profitable gardening to the benefits of maximum planting that can come only with using the carpet method.

 ## THE LONG-LASTING CARPETING AND THE LOW YEARLY COST

The indoor/outdoor carpeting we use on our garden was the subject of a test at Grand Central Station in New York City by the Better Fabrics Testing Bureau. The purpose of this test was to rate how well the carpeting stood up under 1,000,000 foot-traffic passes (73,000 passes is equivalent to one year's heavy use under both indoor and outdoor conditions). The results indicate that this type of carpeting will withstand 15 years of heavy use—and be ready for more. Both appearance and texture had been satisfactorily maintained. (A copy of Report No. 16544 is available from General Felt Industries, Saddle Brook, New Jersey.)

Now, of course, you won't be giving anywhere *near* this kind of wear to the carpeting in your Carpet Garden. Even if *all* your admiring neighbors parade up and down among the rows of vegetables for years and years and years (and we hardly think they will have the time or inclination to do this), your carpeting would still not even come close to having the wear of the carpeting in the Grand Central Station experiment. Actually, the carpeting in your garden will receive hardly any wear at all—certainly no more than any other indoor/outdoor carpeting which is being used as it is intended to be, outdoors. Remember, all you'll be doing will be using it as a mulch. We can only assume that its lifespan should exceed twenty years at the very least. You could probably double that figure if the carpet is rolled up and stored for the winter.

Indoor/outdoor carpeting is available in many different styles, colors (see the discussion of various colors earlier in this chapter), and prices. It is sold in department stores and in carpeting centers all over the country, and we advise you to shop around to get exactly what you want and at the best price.

In the following table, various sample Carpet Gardens have been priced according to size, estimated lifespan, and what you can expect to pay per year for a mulch that will not only look great but will truly eliminate working and worrying.

## THE INDOOR/OUTDOOR CARPET GARDEN GUIDE

| SIZE OF CARPET GARDEN (100% POLYPROPYLENE)* | EQUIVALENT TRADITIONAL TYPE GARDEN† | SUGGESTED CROP PLANTING | COST PER YEAR‡ |
|---|---|---|---|
| | | Strictly for low-growing crops such as lettuce, chard, beets, carrots, onions, etc. | |
| 3′ × 9′ | 6′ × 18′ | | $ .38 |
| 4′ × 12′ | 8′ × 24′ | | .52 |
| 6′ × 9′ | 12′ × 18′ | Suggest slit-type cutouts | .75 |
| 6′ × 12′ | 12′ × 24′ | | 1.00 |
| 9′ × 12′ | 18′ × 24′ | Appropriate size for planting all varieties of vegetables | 1.50 |
| 12′ × 21 | 24′ × 42′ | | 3.50 |
| 12′ × 30′ | 24′ × 60′ | Suggest slit- and hole-type cutouts | 5.00 |
| 15′ × 24′ | 30′ × 48′ | | 5.00 |

*Polypropylene indoor/outdoor carpeting can be purchased in 6-, 12-, and 15-foot widths.
†Actual size of traditional (cultivated) garden necessary to produce as much produce as corresponding Carpet Garden.
‡Actual cost per year based on average retail price of $2.50 per square yard and estimated lifespan of 20 years.

 ## NO BUGS

While the carpet we use on our garden is the least expensive of the indoor/outdoor carpets, we have learned recently that other more expensive carpets manufactured in this country have actually been tested and have been proven to reject black beetle larvae. Not having experimented with such carpeting, we can only say that we have been pleasantly surprised by the near absence of pests in the garden we have today.

Although the bugs in our area may be different from your bugs, it appears that many garden robbers, such as slugs, cutworms, and aphids, just don't like indoor/outdoor carpeting. Possibly they find it strange stuff to crawl on, or maybe it smells bad to them, or perhaps they reason that they can't hide in it. We really don't know —all we do know is that it seems to work! Over the five years that we have been experimenting with the carpet method, we have never planted a traditional garden beside the Carpet Garden to compare the number of bugs or other pests. However, from memory and fair comparison with other gardens in our area, we would definitely say we have far, far less trouble.

## NO ROOT ROT

The type of indoor/outdoor carpeting essential for gardening is that which has *no latex or foam-rubber backing* on it. This type of carpeting is, of course, the least expensive and can be found in any store selling indoor/outdoor carpeting. The lack of backing will permit sufficient air to circulate as well as excessive moisture to evaporate, thus avoiding possible root rot. If you purchase a carpet with a backing on it, we can guarantee that your onions will, indeed, turn to slime!

# CHAPTER 2

# Planning Your Carpet Garden

Vegetables are as different as the people who grow them. Endives are for those who love salads; radishes are for gardeners who want quick results; and carrots are for nibblers and therefore are for us.

Before deciding which vegetables to grow in your Carpet Garden, ask yourself which vegetables you like to eat. Also, which are the favorites of the other people that your Carpet Garden will be feeding?

After you have decided on this, ask yourself if you really plan to, or have the time to, prepare these vegetables for canning or freezing, or if you want just enough to eat freshly picked.

Knowing this will greatly assist you in determining the varieties of vegetables for your garden and in deciding whether you should plant every few weeks or all at once for a big harvest.

To begin, we would recommend avoiding the relatively cheap staples or space-consuming crops such as potatoes. By leaving these out, you will have more room for the real goodies that everyone in the family looks forward to.

Perennials are not for Carpet Gardens, either—that is, if you plan to roll up the garden each fall and store it for the winter. We would suggest that perennials such as asparagus, horseradish, multiplying onions, and rhubarb be situated outside the carpet area for best results. This is because these plants come up wherever they want to, and not necessarily where the holes are. Knowing this, we planted some asparagus a good distance from the garden and spread rock salt around them to keep the weeds down.

Some other plants that don't fare too well in the Carpet Garden are potatoes. With the hilling and digging required, the carpet is in the way. If you must have potatoes, plant them outside the carpet area and use the mulching technique to save on weeding. A word of caution: we have several friends who used hay as mulch and all but one found that it became a haven for mice, which, unseen and safe, gnawed on every potato. We think the best way to have potatoes is either the time-tested hoe and shovel method, or do as we do and buy them. Corn, too, requires hilling and would do best planted outside the carpet area.

Occasionally, confusion arises in distinguishing perennials from annual plants that give volunteer seedlings each year. The best example of such annuals is the tomato, which is a prolific reseeder. Although volunteer plants can be grown to harvest, our experience has been that they never perform like their parents. For this reason, we suggest you begin each season with new plants and forget about the volunteers.

## TIME TO START PLANNING

If you've written for catalogs by January, they'll begin arriving in late winter—your signal to begin planning your garden. Then you'll have plenty of time to do some early indoor sowing of slow-starting seeds.

Seed catalogs contain a wealth of gardening information. In them, you'll find an amazing variety of vegetables: yellow zucchini, the new snowball white tomato, and long fellow cucumbers. You'll see advertisements for compost kits, vegetable slicers, and tree wound dressings, and instructions on how to dry flowers and how to grow your own popcorn.

No matter what you're planning to grow, these catalogs have it all —everything from berries to bulbs to banana melons. Even if you decide to purchase from a local nursery rather than order by mail, the catalogs are great fun to look through and can give you a lot of good ideas. (See page 109 in the appendix for where to send for the catalogs.)

## MINI, MIDI, OR MAXI?

If you are short on tillable ground, the Carpet Garden is just right for you. The carpeting conveniently comes in 6-foot, 12-foot, and 15-foot widths and can be laid out in any combination of these dimensions. (See the many different space arrangements you can make and the various types of layouts in the charts on pages 58–61.) A Carpet Garden will provide plenty of produce for a family of four in a 12-by-15-foot area. (Remember, if properly planned, your garden will provide the equivalent of a 24-by-30-foot traditional garden without wasting a single seed.)

For the family of four with a particular fancy for fresh vegetables, we would recommend the 12-by-25-foot size.

28

Our garden measures 12 feet by 35 feet and we have more vegetables than we can possibly use. In fact, each year we give away armloads of vegetables to our friends. It's so much nicer and more appreciated than the bottle-in-the-bag type of gift. During the winter, we often bring herbs or jarred tomatoes, and the dinner invitations come pouring in.

If you have a family of four or more with a real appetite for fresh greens and also favor the idea of putting up produce for the winter months, we would definitely recommend our 12-by-35-foot size. Instead of one long strip, this size garden can be laid out to measure 17½ feet by 24 feet, using two sections of carpet.

## THE GARDEN PLAN

Assuming that you have decided on the size of Carpet Garden you want, and have armed yourself with a list of vegetables (and how much of each will be planted in the garden), it is now time to begin planning your Carpet Garden, and that means selecting the best possible position for each plant.

The garden plans on pages 58–61 have been prepared to assist you in the proper layout.

We plant our garden in rows running east and west since plants are less likely to shadow one another this way. Not only do we plant our Carpet Garden in an east-west direction, but we place the tallest plants on the north end of the garden and the short, thin plants (like onions) on the south side. The medium-size plants go in the middle rows. This really works for us, and we can tell you right now that "nothing shadows nothing."

## GARDENS ARE FUSSY

Plants are particular about soil, sun, and water. They do extremely well during the season that suits their nature and don't like to be starved or stunted by lack of water, nutrients, or sun.

The following conditions should be met in order to achieve the ultimate in Carpet Gardening success:

1. A successful garden must have at least six hours of sun a day (preferably full sun). Many vegetables prefer sun all day. Normally, the south and west sides of your garden get the most light and heat.

We would suggest that a Carpet Garden in a hot desert area be situated for afternoon shade and that winter gardens in mild-climate areas should have sun all day.

2. Position your garden so as to prevent strong gusts of wind from knocking over staked plants. Natural (hedges) or man-made (walls) barricades on the west and north sides of the garden will deflect the harshest winds. A slope facing southeast will be the most protected.

3. Choose an area where air can circulate. Many plant diseases thrive in stagnant air.

4. Ideally, your garden should be graded slightly higher in the center to promote good surface drainage. If your garden area is too flat or sunken in spots, the entire area could get flooded in a heavy rain. On the other hand, if the slope of the garden is too great, the garden could get washed away. So try to select a graded site or form this slope yourself when working the soil in the spring.

5. If your Carpet Garden is situated near one or more large trees, you are in for a real surprise. The roots of large trees or shrubs are widespreading and will rob the soil of precious moisture and nutrients needed by your vegetables.

## STAY CLOSE TO HOME

It would be wise to locate your garden close to home. Not only will you find it more convenient, but your daily visits will allow you to spot problems as they arise and take care of them.

Skunks, rabbits, and other wild animals can be discouraged if you place your Carpet Garden near the center of domestic activity.

We prefer to fence our garden because we have seen what deer can do to a row of Swiss chard in a matter of seconds. Nothing is more discouraging than to view your garden after it has been wiped out by animals during a midnight raid.

## TAKE SOME CLUES FROM THE
## WEEDS IN YOUR AREA

The conditions of the plants or surrounding shrubs already growing on the proposed site for your garden should tell you something about the existing soil conditions. If the site is overgrown with thick grass and vigorously healthy weeds, the soil beneath is bound to be rich. However, if the soil is too poor to support more than a few anemic weeds and some thin, scraggly grass, then you have to get busy bringing the soil up to a point at which it will provide the ultimate nutrients for your plants—and this will have to be done each year.

# CHAPTER 3

# Preparing the Soil

Preparing the soil is one of the most important steps in gardening. The method you use will be determined by the size of the garden you plant. A small salad or summer garden will probably be worked by hand, using a shovel and fork, whereas a larger garden might require hiring someone to till the soil by mechanical means.

If you are starting a new garden in an area which has never been used before to grow vegetables, we suggest turning over the soil in the fall and leaving any vegetation to decompose and to be broken up by frosts during the winter. Turning under weeds, hay, and grass in the garden area will help to enrich the soil and to improve its texture.

You should begin preparing the soil early in the spring. However, if the ground is still soggy from melting snow or spring rains, it would be wise to wait for it to dry out enough to break apart.

The soil should be loose and friable to a depth of 8 inches. Organic matter should be finely chopped and there should be no large clods or clumps of earth. To accomplish this easily, you might find it worth your while, because of the time and work it saves you, to rent a Rototiller from a hardware store or hire someone with a Rototiller to turn the soil thoroughly for you, for a low fee. The extra work spent tilling, raking, and cultivating the soil will really pay off during the long summer months—remember, once your plants are growing, there is little you can do to improve the texture of the soil.

If you are lucky enough to have a choice parcel of ground in which to put a garden, it could affect the success of your plants for years to come. In this case, you might not have to enrich the soil at all. These ideal conditions include soil that is fertile, well drained, loamy, and relatively free of stones.

Unfortunately, you probably won't be able to choose a garden site with ideal soil, so you'll have to take the best that is available.

## TYPES OF SOILS AND REMEDIES

*Clay soils:* Retain plant foods and moisture, but difficult to work, and warm slowly. Plow in fall and leave rough all winter—easier to handle in spring (expanding ice forces soil apart, making it more friable). It dries out more quickly this way in the spring. Add hydrated lime—initially 5–10 pounds per 100 square feet. If soil is distinctly acid, every 3–5 years add ¼ this amount. It is better to apply after plowing or digging, then cultivate into surface soil. Add sand and sifted wood ashes and compost for best results.

*Peaty soils:* Add lime in large amounts, equal to that applied to clay soils, and liberal applications of commercial fertilizers rich in phosphorus and potash.

*Sandy soils:* Add well-decayed humus. Apply lime—5 pounds to 100 square feet. Do not plow in fall.

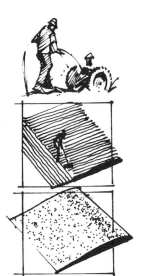

## CARPET GARDEN DRAINAGE

Ideally, every garden should have well-drained subsoil. If puddles form on the garden site, root rot can occur and much damage to plants and fruits will be noticed. This can be overcome by tilting the garden slightly to allow heavy rains to run off.

## YOUR SOIL IS ALIVE!

By "alive," we specifically mean that each square inch of good garden soil contains millions of microorganisms. Although most forms of soil life are too small to be seen, we are all familiar with one of the largest soil organisms, the ordinary earthworm, which feeds entirely upon raw, undigested vegetable matter. In the gradual process of literally consuming and decomposing all dead plant and animal remains, soil organisms cause the release of valuable minerals and trace elements in a form that plant roots can absorb. If you want healthy, fertile, and continuously productive soil, it must be fed plenty of organic matter.

The first step toward successfully preparing the soil for your Carpet Garden or *any type* of garden is to test the soil for "potential of Hydrogen" (pH). The pH of soil is measured on a scale of 1 to 14, 1 being extremely acidic and 14 extremely alkaline.

There are many soil-testing kits on the market that are simple to operate and quite accurate. However, state agricultural colleges provide free soil-testing services and will let you know the fertilizer and lime requirements for your particular crops.

## THE SOIL SAMPLE

To obtain a soil sample, first remove surface debris from the immediate area. Avoiding wet spots, scoop away a section of earth by inserting a shovel 6 inches into the soil and pushing the handle forward. Then, using a tablespoon, take a sample of soil about 3 inches below the surface. Withdraw the shovel and push the soil back into place. Take similar samples from at least 10 points in the garden plot and put them into a container, mixing the soil.

## HOW TO IMPROVE YOUR SOIL

We have noticed that the native acidic soils of the Northeast (where our garden is located) have just the right soil reaction for rhododendrons and azaleas. But vegetables get into trouble when the pH is too low. Vegetables thrive at a pH of 4.9 up to a neutral 7.0. Some vegetables such as lettuce like a pH of 8. However, if your garden soil tests out at 6, you can rest assured that the bulk of your vegetables will do very well.

Chemical analysis shows that a plant may contain as many as 40 elements; however, only 15 are necessary to its normal functioning. Carbon, oxygen, and hydrogen are the three elements that account for about 90 percent of the dry weight of any average plant. Nitrogen, phosphate, and potash are the primary plant foods found in all complete commercial fertilizers. Although they occur in much smaller quantities than the three essential elements (nitrogen is only 1.5 percent of the total dry weight), the primary plant foods have tremendous effects on growth and general health.

If you suspect your soil of being deficient in elements which don't show up in ordinary soil tests, you might want to send a sample to one of the laboratories listed below:

Prescription Soil Analyses
P.O. Box 80631
Lincoln, Nebraska 68501

Soil and Plant Laboratory, Inc.
P.O. Box 153
Santa Clara, California 95052

For symptoms of trace-element deficiencies, consult the following chart:

# KNOW YOUR PLANT FOOD ELEMENTS

| ELEMENT | SYMBOL | FUNCTION IN PLANT | DEFICIENCY SYMPTOMS | EXCESS SYMPTOMS | SOURCES |
|---|---|---|---|---|---|
| Nitrogen | N | Gives plant dark green color. Increases growth in leaf and stem. Makes plant crisp and stimulates early growth. | Light green to yellow leaves. Stunted growth. | Dark green, excessive growth. Retarded maturity. Loss of buds or fruit. | Urea, ammonia nitrates. |
| Phosphorus | P | Stimulates early growth of roots. Gives plant rapid and vigorous start. | Red or purple leaves. Cell division retardation. | Possible tie-up of other essential elements. | Superphosphate, rock phosphate. |
| Potash | K | Increases resistance to plant diseases. Stimulates strong, stiff stalks. Promotes sugar, starch. Increases size. | Reduced vigor. Susceptibility to disease. Thin skin. Small fruit. | Coarseness. Poor coloring. Loss of buds and fruit. | Muriate or sulphate of potash. |

## NEW LIFE FOR OLD GARDENS

As people become more and more interested in gardening, old forgotten gardens are being put to use again. A simple rule of Carpet Garden green thumb seems to work well for a new garden or for one which has lain fallow for 4 or 5 years. First, lime should be spread over the area and worked into the top 4 inches of soil. Next, a complete fertilizer, such as 5–10–10 should be applied at the rate of one 12-quart bucket for every 1,000 square feet. The fertilizer should be mixed into the top 2 or 3 inches of the soil.

The best time to add fertilizer in your Carpet Garden is a day or two before you are going to roll out the carpet and plant. If you fertilize too early, much nitrogen will be lost. It will drift off into the atmosphere as nitrogen gas if it is not used right away.

## FERTILIZER FANTASIES

Once you look at fertilizers from a plant's point of view, one fact is revealed: a plant requires an exceedingly small amount of fertilizer on a continuous basis. Whether you apply enough fertilizer for 60 days at one time, or give what the plant needs for one day is up to the gardener.

We heartily recommend the new timed-release fertilizers over the conventional once-a-month soluble variety. These innovative fertilizers release just what the plant needs, day-by-day, over a 3- to 4-month period. While it is true that they furnish more nutrients when they are first applied than at the end of the period, timed-release fertilizers protect plants from lapses in the gardener's attention.

While some gardeners contend that chemical fertilizers produce inferior vegetables, we find that such beliefs have no practical or scientific foundations. On the other hand, the best possible fertilizer for plants is well-rotted cow manure. We add a pickup truck load of it to our garden every year and the results have been incredible. Fresh manure can be tilled or be Rototilled into the ground in the fall, but well-rotted cow manure should always be used in the spring. Whichever method you choose to use, the end result will be identical in the quality, nutrition, and flavor of your produce.

## COMPOST, THE FERTILIZER THAT PLANTS LOVE

The main purpose of a compost pile is to mix moisture, air, and organic matter in equal amounts to encourage decomposition and form humus as quickly as possible. We collect waste materials, leaves, kitchen scraps, and harvested plants in a compost organizer made of heavy wire mesh, located outside the Carpet Garden.

To get helpful bacteria and fungi working for you within the pile, you need to add a source of protein and nitrogen such as manure, rich soil, alfalfa meal, cottonseed meal, or dry dog food. Any of these activators provides a richer compost system. Commercial fertilizers will not work as activators because the microorganisms you are trying to encourage do not seem to be interested in man-made nitrogen, and they do not seem to generate heat—an essential factor in successful composting.

To start a compost system, first collect whatever organic material you have. This might include leaves, grass clippings, garbage, and rich soil.

Next, build a circular wire cage by fastening together opposite ends of a strip of heavy wire mesh 3 feet wide by 9 feet long.

Start the pile by placing a 2–6-inch layer of leaves, hay, or weeds in the bottom. Then sprinkle on a large handful of activator, thoroughly covering the first layer. Continue building up the compost pile with additional layers of coarse materials such as hay and weeds, alternating layers of high-protein activators.

When the organizer is full, water the pile thoroughly but do not soak it. Most failures in composting are due to the piles' being too dry or too wet.

In approximately one week, the temperature of the pile will reach 140° to 150°F., and you can then begin mixing the pile and adding more water. This will keep the process working for an additional week, at which time the pile will stop heating.

The compost can be stored in the cage until fall, when you roll up the carpet. It should then be mixed with the soil and allowed to decompose during the winter months.

Composting systems can be helpful in preparing soil for more productive plants. However, with the Carpet Garden method, this need only be done every three years.

# CHAPTER 4

# Planting Your Carpet Garden

In the spring, once the soil has been properly prepared and enriched with the necessary fertilizers, the garden area should be thoroughly raked. This will insure a smooth surface on which to place the carpet.

The carpet should then be rolled out over the garden area and pulled to avoid any rolls in the surface area. If you discover bumps on the carpet surface, don't hesitate to tamp them down with your feet. We would recommend wearing sneakers for this job because the soil beneath the carpet area will be soft and it is possible that you could bruise or tear the surface with hard-soled shoes.

One nice thing about working in this kind of garden is that you can do so lying down. It's very comfortable! In time, you'll probably find yourself stretched out in the garden admiring all the young weedless plants during the first months. It's a great place to relax or write a book, as we did. And later, as the plants begin to reach for the sky, you can hold a vegetarian party and invite all the nonbelievers.

We only wish that the climate was such in our neck of the woods that we could spend more time just relaxing in the garden and watching the great performance of harvest year 'round.


**THE FENCE**

Once the carpet is in position, you can begin setting up the fence. The fence will be positioned within the carpet area of the garden approximately 4 inches from the outermost edge of carpet. This is done for a very good reason—the fence, as you will see, plays a very important role in the planning of the Carpet Garden.

Not only will the fence keep out the animals that will attempt to eat your plants and vegetables (as we've told you, deer are crazy about Swiss chard), but the fence can also be used to support many plants that would ordinarily take up considerable space on the carpet, thus reducing the maximum planting potential by 30 percent.

Plants such as melons, cucumbers, and tomatoes love hanging on the fence, and it makes harvesting so much easier because you don't have to bend over to pick them. By keeping these vegetables off the ground and on the fence, you won't have to worry about surface contact, which can bruise certain vegetables. Also, think of the better exposure to sunlight they will get, hanging high on the fence.

## WHAT KIND OF FENCE?

We recommend using heavy wire fencing, the kind with rectangular holes about 2 inches in size. We admit this can be a bit costly, but again, it lasts as long as the carpet and that can be a very long time. If the cost is too high, however, the small-holed chicken-wire fencing we use works fine, but you'll have a bit of a time straightening it in the fall for your next garden. It's amazing what melons, cucumbers, and tomato plants can do to light wire fencing. (For instructions on fencing, see pages 52–53.)

## CUTTING YOUR GARDEN CARPET

### The Cutouts

There are two basic types of cuts that are made in the Carpet Garden: the *slit* and the *circular cut.*

The slit type of cut measures 1 inch in width and no more than 3 feet in length, and the circular cut never exceeds 3 inches in diameter.

We're sure you won't have any trouble cutting out the slits. A chalkline is helpful for aligning the various rows of slits, as well as the rows of holes. And a yardstick can serve as a guide for marking off the rows and enable you to cut parallel lines on both sides of the stick.

The circle cuts are a bit more difficult, however. We've always used a large milk glass as a guide and, by holding it firmly on the carpet, you will be able to run a paring knife or blade around the contour of the glass, thus producing a perfect circle cutout. However, you may prefer to use an electric drill with a hole-cutting attachment.

We find that the circle cutouts should be just large enough to accommodate the individual plants, and under no circumstances should you need holes larger than two to three inches. Any large plant not planted from seed, such as eggplant, broccoli, or cauli-

42

flower, should get along just fine in the three-inch circle cutouts. The holes for peppers and some squash can be made smaller because they are not as thick-stemmed as broccoli is, for example.

### Circles and Slits

After positioning the fence posts and securing the wire mesh properly, you're ready to cut. With the aid of a chalk line indicate where the first row of plants will be located. In fact, before cutting any holes or slits in the carpet, it would be wise to indicate with chalk where everything is to go.

We suggest beginning at the north end of the garden where the tall, climbing plants will be positioned. This row of plants will require only circular cutouts.

Be sure to follow carefully your original plan or the plans which have been prepared for this book. Remember, you have a real investment in the carpet, so let's not make a mess of it.

The first cut is always scary on a new carpet, but after the first two or three, you'll get the knack.

### Saving the Cutouts

Because we are basically lazy, and also because we don't want to waste anything, we hang onto the carpet strips and circles cut from the carpet.

We do this so that when we plant rows of lettuce, for example, we can plant one-third of a row at a time and, 2 or 3 weeks later, can plant an additional third of a slit.

The carpet cutouts are used to cover any portion of a slit which has not yet been planted, to keep out weeds.

As you have guessed by now, *we just hate to weed!*

## PLANT SPACING

Traditionally, lots of space is left between rows of plants to facilitate weeding and cultivation. A space of at least 18 inches is needed to ensure that the plants are not damaged by cultivating tools. However, with the Carpet Garden method, this phase of garden maintenance is obsolete because there's virtually no way weeds can grow in the garden area. Consequently, these valuable 18 (and more) inches can now be used to grow additional produce, especially in the area used for low-growing plants.

Tomato plants can be positioned as close together as 10 inches without limiting their supply of sunshine or nutrients. This includes all varieties except for cherry tomatoes, which can be planted at 6-inch intervals. Three to 5 plants will supply an average four-mem-

ber family, but go ahead and plant more if you plan to put them up or give them away. We put our cherry tomatoes against the north fence because they need support, although they could be staked in the middle of the garden.

Beans, muskmelons, and other climbers are also best positioned on the north fence.

Due to the size of these plants, move 3 feet south of the north fence and begin the next east-west row with medium-size plants such as eggplant, cauliflower, and broccoli. We plant ours 18 inches apart; however you could reduce this to 12 inches.

Go another 3 feet and plant the third row. Here's a really good place for peppers or anything else that grows about 2 feet high.

So far we've been spacing out the various rows of plants at 3-foot intervals. The reason for this has to do not only with the sun but with the fact that the plants we've been suggesting need a lot of room to grow.

We would suggest that you follow this 3-foot-interval method of plant spacing in your first year of Carpet Gardening rather than attempting to plant at maximum potential right away. By taking this first season to become familiar with the size and maturing height of vegetables grown in your climate region, you will be better prepared to cut additional rows of slits and holes the following summer. You will find that you can plant closer and closer together in the following years. We have experimented with mass Carpet Garden planting for a more profitable harvest and the results have been incredible! Although such mass planting considerably reduces the walking space between the rows in the garden, you will still be able to make your way through the garden because vegetables mature at different rates. If you want to store vegetables over the winter, you may want to practice closer planting and accept happily any slight inconvenience in walking among your garden's delicious profusion!

The south end of the garden is where the smallest plants, such as radishes, lettuce, onions, chard, and herbs, are grown. At this end of the Carpet Garden, you will only have to be concerned about cutting slits, because all of these small vegetables do best when planted this way.

It is on the south side of the garden that you can really economize on space. We would plant this area in such a way as to have 3 rows of slits contained within 1 foot of space.

Notice that the slits in the photograph are about 3 feet long, then there is a 1-foot space, then there are 3 more slits, and so on. It is important that you leave a 1-foot space between the rows of slits. This is planned so that the carpet will have more strength to withstand being rolled up for storage in the fall.

Since peas can be planted less than 1 inch apart, we suggest that a long slit 1 inch wide be cut for them.

44

## THE PLANTS

You may disagree, but we feel that, unless you have a greenhouse or a cold frame and some expertise, it is a sheer waste of time, money, and energy to grow your own tomato, pepper, and other plants from seed. Doing it yourself means buying potting soil, seeds, peat pots, trays, having to water and tend them for many weeks, and ultimately finding yourself with a handful of frail, leggy plants.

Why not just forget about all that do-it-yourself stuff and let the professionals handle the plants? For just a few dollars you can buy plants that will be strong and bursting with energy. We promise that you'll have much better results.

If you plan to go with greenhouse plants entirely, then we suggest you look around for a good source and get to know the owner. He's a good friend to have and can really save you lots of time figuring out the best selection of plants for your garden.

You'll find out which plants are successful in your soil and climate, what's good that's new, and what plants to avoid. And he'll probably advise buying hybrids—they're more disease-resistant and yield more and better fruit than standard varieties.

When the time comes to place these plants in the Carpet Garden, the transplanting shock is considerably less than that received by plants in the traditional garden. This is due to the carpet's ability to keep the soil warm during early spring nights and days. The shock, nevertheless, usually results in slow growth for several weeks. Soon this will pass and your garden will burst into vigorous growth.

## STAKING

For plants that need staking, such as tomatoes, pole beans, eggplants and most peppers, it is best to put in the stakes when you plant. If you stake later when the plant needs it, there's a good chance you'll break the roots.

The stake should always be placed in the same cutout used for the plant.

The best kind of wire and paper Twist-ems to secure the plant to the stake are those that come on a large roll. They are not only cheapter bought uncut, but you can make them as long or as short as you want.

## THINNING

When the peas are harvested and the cauliflower is cut, the plants should be pulled out. If you happen to be thinning lettuce, onions,

or Swiss chard, why not place a plant in a vacant hole? If no thinning is to be done, then simply cover the hole with the cutouts you've been saving.

## WATERING THE GARDEN

We promised ourselves we wouldn't mention the word "water" because we are thoroughly convinced that Carpet Gardens require no water other than that provided by Mother Nature.

However, if some morning you have nothing to do (a common state among Carpet Gardeners) or if the weather has been very, very dry for a long time, then pick up the hose and give the garden a little water.

## INSECTS

We personally have found very few insects in our garden over the past five years. We've rarely dusted and have not yet had a serious problem. We get the feeling that bugs find the carpet very inhospitable.

Some of this good fortune may be due to the marigolds we plant around the garden to repel insects. Other plants that are known to deter or repel insects are listed below. If you wish to add some insurance against ever having an insect problem in your garden, you may wish to choose some plants from this list to put in or around your garden. Many, like the marigolds, go around the carpet area but not in it, and make very attractive borders. Others, such as the eggplant and tomato, go right in the Carpet Garden.

*PLANTS THAT DETER OR REPEL INSECTS*

| Aster | Deters most insects |
| Basil | Repels both mosquitoes and flies |
| Borage | Deters tomato worms |
| Calendula | Deters most insects |
| Catnip | Deters flea beetles |
| Chrysanthemum | Deters most insects |
| Eggplant | Deters Colorado potato beetle |
| Flax | Deters potato bug |
| Garlic | Deters Japanese beetle and other insects |
| Geranium | Repels most insects |
| Horseradish | Deters potato bug |
| Marigold | The very best of all pest deterrents, particularly nematodes, if planted with onions |

46

| | |
|---|---|
| Mint | Deters ants |
| Mole plant | Deters mice and moles |
| Onions | Deters most pests |
| Petunia | Protects beans from many insects |
| Peppermint | Repels cabbage butterfly |
| Radish | Great for repelling cucumber beetle |
| Rosemary | Deters bean beetle and carrot fly |
| Sage | Deters cabbage moth and carrot fly |
| Salsify | Repels carrot fly |
| Savory | Deters bean beetle |
| Tomato | Repels asparagus beetle |
| Thyme | Deters cabbage worm |

## CARPET GARDEN COMPANION PLANTS

The following is a list of vegetables that make good companions when planted in the same garden. If both plants are not planted at the same time, the crop listed first should be planted first. Using this method will bring about higher productivity and will help ward off bugs.

| | |
|---|---|
| Peas and carrots | Corn and spinach |
| Cabbage and lettuce | Corn and lettuce |
| Carrots and radishes | Tomatoes and spinach |
| Onions and radishes | Tomatoes and radishes |
| Parsnips and radishes | Tomatoes and lettuce |
| Cabbage and radishes | Swiss chard and peppers |
| Cabbage and onion sets | Onion sets and radishes |
| Lettuce and chives | Cabbage and sage |
| Peas and chives | Squash and radishes |

## CARPET GARDEN ROTATION

If you planned your garden in an east-west direction for least shadowing, we don't see why the same vegetables have to be planted in the same places year after year. As you probably already know, this is a bad practice, even if you do fertilize, Rototill, and compost each spring.

If you've planted tomatoes at one end of the north fence your first year, in the second summer, why not move the tomatoes to the center position and move the cucumbers to the left or right of the tomatoes? The same method of rotation can be exercised in all the east-west rows by simply changing the position of vegetables within the row.

47

## HARVESTING

One of the nicest things about harvesting vegetables from your Carpet Garden is that they are so nice and clean. We have never seen Swiss chard so free of dirt. Anyone who has ever tried to thoroughly clean any of these curly, leafy plants under the faucet knows what a challenge it is to get rid of all the grit. In ordinary gardens, quite a bit of soil sloshes up every time it rains and coats the leaves of the tender greens. Lovely, clean vegetables are just another of the great benefits of the Carpet Garden.

One of the nicest problems is having so much produce that it is hard to find it all. Harvesting is a never-ending event! One thing we have noticed in growing the tall, viny plants on the north fence is that, because of the size of some of the leaves, such as those of cucumbers and beans, and the green color of the vegetables themselves, we have a devil of a time finding all the produce.

Several times we have been in the garden and made a little game out of picking the cucumbers. We search our best and pick all we can that are longer than, say, six inches. Then we leave the garden and walk around to the back of the north fence. Every time, we find several we have missed.

## CARPET CARE

We would definitely recommend storing your carpet for the winter months, right from the start. This will greatly extend its life and that of your gardening investment.

To do this, all that is needed is to pull out the remaining plants in the fall, remove the fence, and roll up the carpet. Before storing it, hang it on a sturdy clothes line and allow it to dry thoroughly. You can then leave it in an attic, basement, garage, or shed over the winter and get busy turning over the soil in preparation for your next year's Carpet Garden.

Fertilizer analysis numbers refer to percentages by weight. The three major elements are always listed by number in this order: nitrogen, phosphorus, and potash.

Photographs at right illustrate the proper procedure for laying out the carpet.

The Rototiller is the gardener's best friend for help in soil preparation. A Rototiller can be rented or you can hire someone to till.

# Roll Out the Garden

Once the carpet has been rolled out over the soil surface, it should be thoroughly watered. This initial watering should last for approximately 3 minutes per square yard of carpet to assure sufficient moisture for plants to grow during the long summer months.

Fence posts must be located 4 inches within the carpet area. This will prevent strong wind gusts from lifting the carpet and will also prevent garden varmints from entering the garden by tunneling under the fence.

A series of 2-inch slits must be cut to allow the fence posts to go through the carpet. The posts should then be driven into the soil until they are rigid. If light wire fencing is being used, a wire spike is needed to anchor the

# Fencing-In the Carpet Garden

fencing in the space between the posts. If rigid fencing is used, this will not be necessary.

Generally a 3- to 4-foot fence surrounding the garden should be high enough to keep deer and other large animals from raiding the garden. However, the north fence must be twice that height to allow ample room and support for the climbing plants.

After installing the posts and fencing, you will be ready to cut the slits and holes where the various plants are to be positioned. The plans on pages 58–61 will give you a variety of suggested layouts.

The tools required to make the cuts are simple ones. All you need are a paring or utility knife, a glass or other circular object measuring approximately 2-½ inches in diameter, and a piece of string to make sure the rows are straight. For slit cuts, a wooden yardstick can be used as a pattern.

If you wish, you can use an electric drill with a hole cutter for circle openings in the carpet. However, the fabric cuts very easily and can be done simply with a sharp paring knife.

# Cutting the Garden Carpet

First scoop enough soil from beneath the carpet hole to allow space for the root structure of the young plant. You can then insert the plant and fill the hole with soil, pressing it into position. If young plants are started in peat pots, they will fit into the circle cutouts.

Where seeds are used in slit cutouts at the south end of the garden, the soil should be gently pushed aside when planting. Once the seeds have been distributed, they should be covered with amounts of soil equal in depth to four times the diameter of the seed.

# Planting the Carpet Garden

In areas not yet planted, position the pieces cut from the slit or circle over the openings to prevent weeds from growing in. You should save these cutout pieces for the purpose of plugging the openings when needed.

Thinning out of plants in the slit cutouts will be necessary from time to time. Rather than just throwing away thinnings, you can transplant some into holes and slits left vacant by earlier harvestings.

# A COMPARISON OF TWO 12-BY-30-FOOT CARPET GARDENS

The diagram on the left represents the first-year spacing techniques for the beginning gardener. The diagram on the right illustrates the maximum potential planting as carried out in the Downers Grove comparison test we performed.

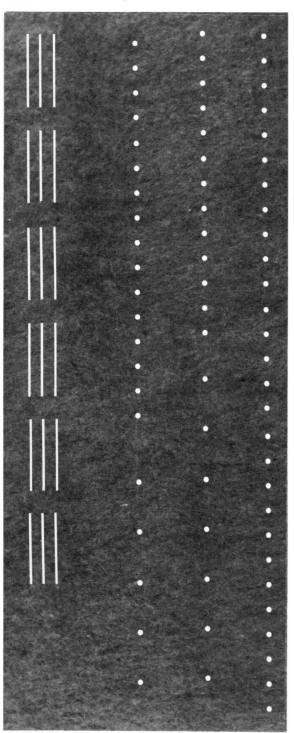 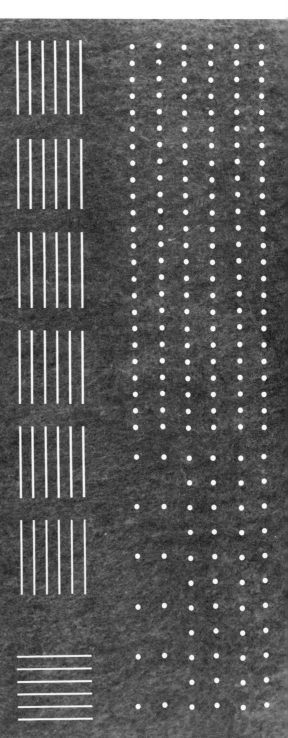

One-quarter inch equals 1 foot in actual size.

## THE 4-BY-12-FOOT
## CARPET GARDEN

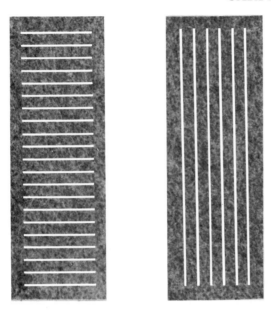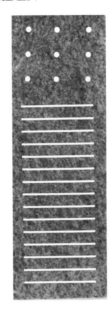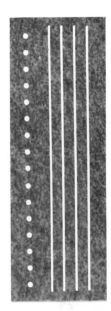

One-quarter inch equals 1 foot in actual size.

## THE 15-BY-24-FOOT
## CARPET GARDEN

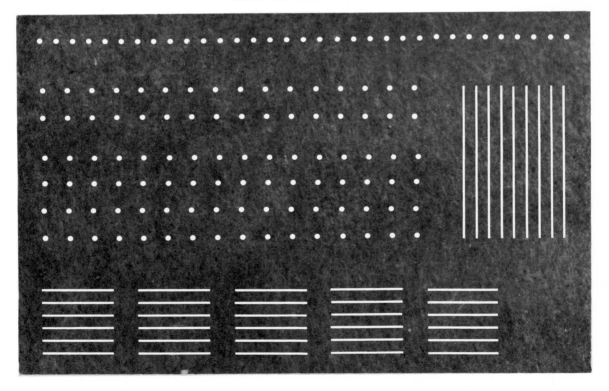

One-quarter inch equals 1 foot in actual size.

### THE 9-BY-12-FOOT
### CARPET GARDEN

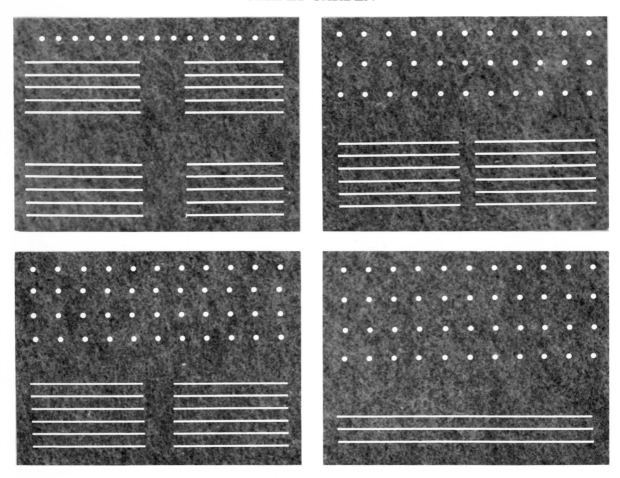

### THE 9-BY-24-FOOT
### CARPET GARDEN

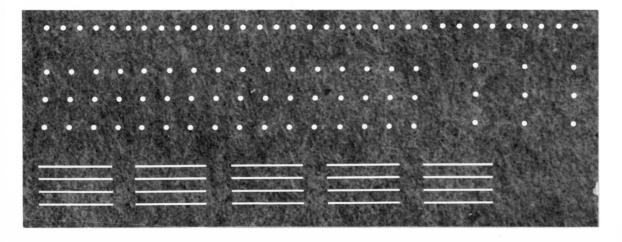

## THE 12-BY-21-FOOT
## CARPET GARDEN

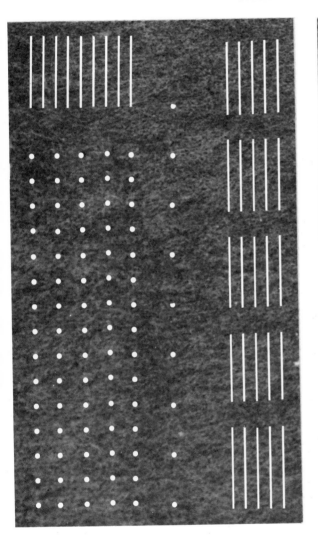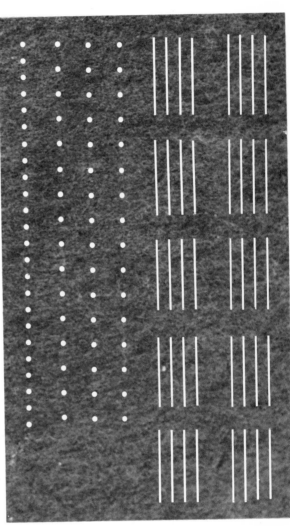

One-quarter inch equals 1 foot in actual size.

# CHAPTER 5

# What to Do with Nature's Bounty

We are not kidding when we say you may have more vegetables than you know what to do with. This is a common problem with Carpet Gardens—and, oh, what a lovely problem it is! As we have said, you will find yourself giving away armloads of beautiful produce to friends and neighbors. And in winter, we find that the best hostess gifts are our own jarred vegetables—not only are the bright colors cheery, but the tastes are a gourmet's delight. You probably also have a normal desire to stock your own larder. So, whether you choose to give away most of your cornucopia or keep it all on your own shelves, we suggest the methods listed below for dealing with all the produce you don't use right away. (For more detailed information in chart form, see The Carpet Gardener's Vegetable Storage Guide in this chapter. Also see the Harvesting-Storage entries under each vegetable in Chapter Six, The Carpet Gardener's Vegetable Guide. Specific storage instructions for individual vegetables, such as turnips, may be found there.)

1. *Storing in root cellars or cold cellars.* Vegetables that store well this way include cabbage, carrots, turnips, beets, cauliflower, broccoli, radishes, squashes, and, of course, onions.

2. *Freezing.* Whether you have one of those big, professional-size freezers or the ordinary little kind in your refrigerator, you can freeze some of your favorite vegetables very successfully. We recommend the following for suitability to freezing: peas, lima beans, string beans, broccoli, cauliflower, chard, and spinach. We suggest that you freeze your vegetables in small amounts only. Once you have defrosted a batch, you should not refreeze it, so only freeze in one package what you think you will use at one time.

Herbs can also be frozen very nicely. Again, freeze in individual batches just what you will need to cook a particular dish. An ideal

way to do this is to place just enough chopped herbs for individual recipes or seasonings for particular dishes in the compartments of plastic ice-cube trays. You can freeze each herb portion in a little bit of water. At cooking time, it is very easy to pick out a cube of your chosen herb and simply drop it right into what you are cooking. The cube melts right away leaving the garden-fresh herb to season what you are preparing.

3. *Canning.* Putting up vegetables in jars takes a little more care than the first two methods. It is very important that you get proper canning instructions (you may get them by writing the U.S. Department of Agriculture, for instance) and follow them religiously. Faulty canning can result in tainted food, as you probably know, so please be careful. Suggested vegetables for preserving this way include tomatoes, peppers, lima beans, string beans, and beets. We find canning very satisfying and really enjoy seeing our vegetables so nicely put up.

Not only will you find that storing your vegetables is economical, but you will also find it to be a great way to cheer up your family's meals. It is so nice on some damp, gray, March day to bring out such lovely vegetables to spark your spirits and to remind you that the days of the great outdoors are coming soon. Eating your own vegetables that you have preserved yourself gives a tremendous feeling of satisfaction and sense of accomplishment. And when you bring your preserved vegetables as gifts to friends, your sensation of pride is nearly intoxicating!

64

# THE CARPET GARDENER'S VEGETABLE STORAGE GUIDE

| VEGETABLE | ROOT CELLAR OR COOL ROOM | DRYING | SALTING | CANNING | FREEZING |
|---|---|---|---|---|---|
| Artichokes | | | | | |
| Asparagus | | | | X | X |
| Beans (all kinds) | | X | X | X | X |
| Beets | X | X | | X | X |
| Broccoli | | X | X | X | X |
| Brussels sprouts | | | | X | X |
| Cabbage | X | X | X | | |
| Carrots | X | X | | X | X |
| Cauliflower | | | | X | X |
| Celery | X | | X | X | |
| Corn | X | X | | X(cooked) | X(cooked) |
| Endive | X | | | | |
| Greens | | X | | X | X |
| Herbs | | X | | | X |
| Kale | | X | X | | X |
| Mushrooms | | X | | X | X |
| Okra | | X | | X | X |
| Onions | X | X | | X | X |
| Parsnips | X | X | | X | X |
| Peas | | X(mature) | | X | X |
| Peppers | | X | | X | X |
| Potatoes (white) | X | | | X | X |
| Potatoes (sweet) | X | X | | X | X |
| Pumpkins | X | | | X | X |
| Rutabagas | X | X | X | X | X |
| Salsify | X | | | | |
| Squash | X | | | X | X |
| Tomatoes | X | | | X | X |
| Turnips | X(waxed) | | X | X | X |

65

# TEMPERATURES, CONDITIONS, AND LENGTH OF STORAGE

| VEGETABLE | FREEZING POINT | STORAGE PLACE | STORAGE TEMPERATURE | STORAGE HUMIDITY | LENGTH OF STORAGE |
|---|---|---|---|---|---|
| Dry beans and peas Late cabbage | 30.4 | Any cool, dry place | 32° to 40° | Dry | Late fall and winter |
| Cauliflower | 30.3 | Cellar | 35° | Dry | 6 to 8 weeks |
| Celery | 31.6 | Trench; roots in soil | 35° | Dry | 6 to 8 weeks |
| Endive Onions Parsnips | 32° | Cellar | 35° | Dry | 2 to 3 months |
| Peppers | 30.7 | Unheated basement or room | 45° to 50° | Slightly moist | 2 to 3 weeks |
| Potatoes | 30.9 | Trench, pit, or cellar | 35° | Slightly moist | Fall and winter |
| Winter squashes | 30.5 | Unheated basement or room | 55° | Slightly moist | Fall and winter |
| Tomatoes (green) | 31° | Unheated basement or room | 55° to 70° | Dry | 4 to 6 weeks |

# CHAPTER 6

# The Carpet Gardener's Vegetable Guide

You may not know *beans* about vegetables, but this guide will soon make you as much of an expert as you'll ever need to be. As you will see, we have taken a commonsense approach to vegetables—we tell you which are the easiest to grow and which are the most difficult; which will deliver the fastest harvest and which the slowest; which are practically free of problems and which almost ask for trouble.

As we have told you earlier, the important thing in choosing vegetables to plant is to decide which ones you really enjoy eating. Quite simply, it is a matter of taste. Remember that your garden is for *you*. But, even if you are really crazy about a certain vegetable, you may have to face the fact that it is impossible to grow in your particular climate, no matter how you try. This is why it is a very good idea to make friends with some old-timers who have been gardening in your area since before you were born. If *they* don't grow a certain vegetable in your area, it is probably for a very good reason. Or ask your local greenhouse owner for suggestions on what and when to plant.

During the season, it's a good idea to keep a record of your gardening activities, such as planting dates, when the first vegetables appear, and how long the harvest lasts. It will be invaluable in planning next year's Carpet Garden. Be sure to refer to our Carpet Gardener's Easy Planting Chart on pages 113–117 for detailed information.

And now, on to our garden of delights. . . .

## BASIL

If you had to limit your herb usage, basil would be one of the few herbs kept. It's so easy to grow, dry, and store that to buy already-dried basil leaves is really just plain silly. You can raise enough basil in one slit-type cutout to last you three years.

### RECOMMENDED VARIETIES

Sweet Basil
Dark Opal (ornamental, but fine for cooking)

### HOW TO GROW

Plant the seeds in slits at the south end of the garden. With proper pruning, they will attain a height of 1½ feet. Thin the plants to about 4 inches apart. When they grow to be about 6 inches in height, pinch them back a good 3 inches. This will cause them to fork and become sturdier. Continue pinching back all new growth.

### HARVESTING, DRYING

To harvest, cut each plant at ground level and bring it indoors. String a cord in any dry, airy room and hang the plants so that they do not touch. Most pieces will be forked, so just invert them for hanging. If there is no fork, the first leaf will be strong enough to support the clipping. As they dry, the leaves and stems will begin to droop, so you'll soon be able to place them even closer together, making room for additional basil. In a few weeks, the leaves should be dry enough to be placed in a jar. After a few days, look to see if any moisture has condensed on the inside of the jar. If it has, remove the basil or it may mildew. Dry it on newspaper for a few days and then return it to the jar.

## BEANS

There are many different kinds of beans, so check the seed packets in case the varieties you choose differ greatly from this generalized guide. Bear in mind that there are two basic kinds of beans grown in most gardens: snap (including wax) and lima. These are divided into two types: pole and bush. Most beans with which you will deal are contained within these four varieties.

### RECOMMENDED VARIETIES

Bush, Lima: Fordhook 242, Thaxter
Pole, Lima: Fordhook, Sieva
Bush, Green: Provider, Tender crop, Topcrop (Early)
Bush, Snap: King Horn, Cherokee
Pole, Green: Kentucky Wonder, Romano

## HOW TO GROW

Wait until the soil warms up to 65° before planting. This may be a bit difficult for you to tell the first year, so why not check with the old-timer whom we hope you have befriended? He might say something like "Wait till the oaks and hickories uncurl their new leaves." And he will have hit the nail on the head again. We suggest that you plant the pole and bush beans along the north fence, about 4 inches apart. For pole beans, fasten sticks or poles vertically against the fence with ties or wire. Don't plant them all at one time. Try several batches, 2 to 3 weeks apart. An important rule of green thumb: do nothing to bean plants while they are wet.

## HARVESTING

Pick the beans while they are young and tender. Frequent picking means a greater yield. Pick them when they start showing lumps from the seeds inside. Be sure not to wait too long. Harvest lima beans before they whiten. If you gather more than you can eat immediately, dry them in the sun until they whiten and store them unshelled in jars. They will keep for many weeks.

## BEETS

Beets are a little slow to start from seed, but once germinated, they grow rapidly and produce a great deal of delicious food in a small space.

Even if you don't like beets, you may find you like the greens; some people plant beets just for the greens. If you have the space, why not plant a spring and a fall crop? Beets are not for summer growing, and with two crops you can store all winter those grown in the fall. Why not start these inside, a few weeks before planting time, in order to have an early crop in the spring?

## RECOMMENDED VARIETIES

Detroit Dark Red
Ruby Queen
Firechief
Formanova (large cylindrical roots)
Burpee's Golden
Green Top Bunching (great for beet-green lovers)

## HOW TO GROW

Beets belong in the slit-type cutouts, at the south end of the Carpet Garden. The seeds, which are quite large, are sometimes planted 3 inches apart. In the Carpet Garden, they can be planted as close as 1 inch apart and about 1 inch deep. If you grow them for greens only, you can plant them even closer, if you wish. You will notice that the sprouting plants seem to be more than you planted. Each seed will have from 4 to even 6 seedlings. Thin them to at least 2 inches apart when the plants are small, using the greens of the small plants.

73

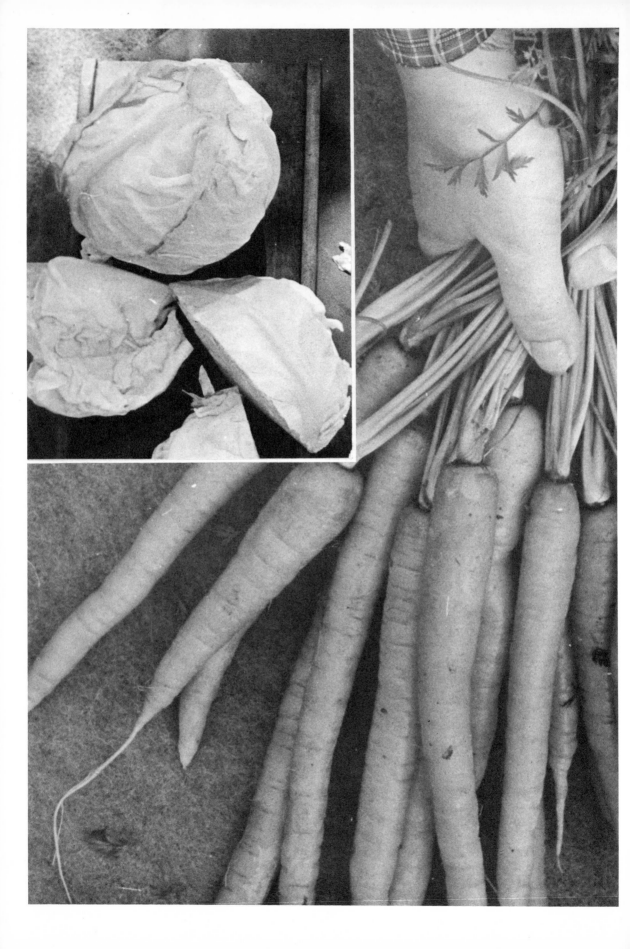

Beets will mature from seed to harvest in approximately 45-60 days. However, they have little tolerance for hot weather and should be planted early or in the fall. It is possible to grow winter crops of beets in the Carpet Garden if yours is located in a mild climate region. In this case, the seeds should be sown in early fall and the roots harvested before they begin to shoot up seed stalks the following spring.

If, for any reason, the weather has been exceptionally dry, we would recommend occasional watering. This will keep the roots tender and plump.

### HARVESTING

Begin pulling whole beet plants when they reach 1 inch in diameter and begin picking greens when the leaves are from 5 to 8 inches tall. This will make room for the remaining beets to mature to 2 or 3 inches. Then you should really start pulling them in earnest. Although the big globes are impressive, it is not wise to allow beets to grow to jumbo size because they will develop woody streaks. Store them as you would potatoes.

## BROCCOLI

Not a season goes by that we don't plant broccoli in our Carpet Garden. It's one of the real favorites and we never share it with neighbors and friends who show up, carrying empty paper bags, just to say hello. We don't mean to sound stingy, but the vegetables all look so tempting in the Carpet Garden that even the most considerate of friends can't help but ask for a few samples. This is definitely a problem you'll run into with your first Carpet Garden and we strongly suggest that you put up a sign which reads:

PLEASE DON'T FEED THE NEIGHBORS
—The Vegetables

### RECOMMENDED VARIETIES
Waltham 29, Green Comet, De Cicco, Coastal, Neptune

### HOW TO GROW

If you want to start in the spring, we would suggest putting in large, strong plants early. In this way, you will be harvesting before the very hot weather. Wrap the stems with wax paper or foil to discourage cutworms. If you take our advice, you will also plant the broccoli by seed (less expensive) in May or June. This fall crop will bear through light frosts. A mid-garden spot is fine, because broccoli grows just a bit more than 2 feet high.

### HARVESTING

Harvest when the buds are still tight. When they start loosening, and the flowers begin to form, you have waited too long and have lost

75

some of the flavor. Harvest the main head, but leave the smaller side shoots. They will get larger and taste just fine. Keep harvesting the plant in this manner because it will encourage the growth of the side shoots.

## CABBAGE

Cabbage is delicious when it is from your own garden; you will be pleasantly surprised by how different its flavor is from that of its supermarket cousin. It is available in many varieties, both red and green, and from plain-leafed to crinkly.

### RECOMMENDED VARIETIES

Early Miniatures: Dwarf Morden, Earliana
Mid-Season: Resistant Golden Acre, Early Jersey Wakefield, Emerald Cross, Harvester Queen, Greenback, King Cole, Salad Green (for cole slaw)
Red: Red Head, Ruby Ball
Late Maturing: Premium Flat Dutch, Savoy Chieftain

### HOW TO GROW

You should buy spring cabbage as plants so that you can give your schedule a 3- to 4-week boost. Grow the fall varieties from seed after midsummer.

Cabbage should be planted in the hole cutouts and spaced approximately 12 inches apart. This vegetable will respond favorably to the cool, moist soil conditions produced by the indoor/outdoor carpet mulch.

### HARVESTING

When the heads are firm and about the size of a softball, it is time to begin harvesting. Cut the stem just beneath the head. Although the cabbage does well in cool weather and a light frost will do it no harm, you should not allow the heads to freeze before harvesting. The heads can be shielded from freezing for several weeks by snapping off some of the outer leaves and covering the head during cold nights.

## CARROTS

Carrots are a cool-season crop so you might run into trouble raising them, depending on your climate region. If you are in doubt, check with your local nursery to determine how well this crop does in your area.

### RECOMMENDED VARIETIES

Nantes, Pioneer, Trophy, Royal Chantenay, Gold Pak

### HOW TO GROW

Carrots go in slits at the south end of the Carpet Garden. The seeds are so very fine that it might be a good idea to mix them with some dry earth so that you do not have to do as much thinning.

Sow them in early spring and thin to about 3 inches apart. Because carrots are so dependent on loose soil and will grow straight and long only if the soil is carefully screened, we plant them along with our radishes. The reason for this is that the radish crop comes up very quickly and helps to break up the soil's crust, allowing the carrots room to stretch their long legs.

If you choose to do it this way, be careful doing the little weeding required in the slit area because carrot seedlings look so grasslike. You might prefer to start them in containers and transplant them as soon as they sprout.

For a constant crop, plant the seedlings every 3 weeks.

### HARVESTING

Don't wait for the carrots to get to the size of prize winners because they will only get coarse. The best-tasting carrots are picked when they are small and sweet. Don't let yours attain a diameter larger than a quarter.

## CAULIFLOWER

Cauliflower can be harvested in cooler weather—in early summer or late fall. If the weather turns hot, it will flower rapidly. It is frost-hardy and needs 60–80 days to reach maturity.

Blanching or whitening of heads can be accomplished by shielding them from the light. To do this, simply gather up the longer outer leaves and fasten them at the top of the head with a wide rubber band.

### RECOMMENDED VARIETIES

Snowball
Snow King Hybrid
Purple Head (This has large plants with heads that are deep purple and turn green when cooked. It tastes rather like broccoli and does not require blanching.

### HOW TO GROW

Cauliflower can be started from small plants. Position them in the hole cutouts 12 to 14 inches apart. If the weather turns quite hot, overhead sprinkling will give the cauliflowers the humidity they need, but be sure not to soak them.

### HARVESTING

You must harvest the heads before the florets begin to separate. Simply cut them off at the stems, just below their heads.

79

## CHARD (SWISS)

This cousin to the beet produces only leaves for eating—but oh, such fine eating! We use it as you would spinach, and, undoubtedly, once you've tried these tender greens, you'll never stop growing them in your Carpet Garden.

One nice thing about growing Swiss chard—true also of many of the other leafy vegetables that will find a place in your garden—is that you will never have to contend with any grit. When you have the Carpet Garden, there is no chance for the heavy rains of summer to bounce up and carry soil into the tender leaves of your plants.

Plan to have at least 6 to 10 plants per family, depending on your taste for chard.

### RECOMMENDED VARIETIES

Rhubarb Chard, Large White Ribbed, Fordhook Giant

### HOW TO GROW

Plant the seeds as soon as the soil can be worked. Chard can bear several frosts, so plan on a long growing season. We plant them about 8 inches apart in slits. You might want to be super lazy and plant them in holes, but we find that the slit-type cutouts work best at the south end of the garden.

For proper rotation of crops, be sure to plant chard in different slits the following years.

### HARVESTING

When harvesting, be sure to cut only the outermost leaves close to the carpet surface. The plant will keep providing leaves, but don't let them get too large because they tend to get stringy.

## CHIVES

Don't let the need that vichyssoise has for chives scare you. Try using them in such mundane dishes as eggs and salad, and you will find out how elegant this member of the onion family can be.

Plan exactly where you want it in the garden, because it is a perennial. You will not only have it from year to year, but you will find that it graces your garden with lovely blossoms. Chives are also nearly disease-free. We have not found enough varieties to make a recommendation; those we've tried have all been successful.

### HOW TO GROW

Although you can start these easily from seed, you might want to start them indoors and move them to the garden when it grows warm. In a few years, the clusters that have developed should be separated and perhaps spread to other places. We put chives in pots and give them to friends as gifts because the plants will keep through the winter.

### HARVESTING

Cut a few leaves from each plant as you need them and then snip them with scissors to the required length. Pot a few clusters and bring them in for winter use.

### CUCUMBER

Both salads and pickling demand the cucumber. It is easy to grow and a few plants will satisfy the needs of any family. Have up to 10 plants if you really love to pickle.

### RECOMMENDED VARIETIES

For slicing: Gemini, Sweet Slice, Marketmore 70, Pacer
For pickling: Green Star, Mariner, Pixie, Pioneer, Crispy

### HOW TO GROW

Plant the seeds when the ground turns warm and the night temperatures are at least 40 degrees. Place 4 seeds to a hole and then thin to 2 plants. If you want to have the first cucumbers, start them indoors in peat pots a few weeks before the last frosts. The pots slip easily into the holes with no damage to the tender roots. Plant them on the north side next to the fence and fasten them every few feet with ties.

### HARVESTING

As with many vegetables, old fruit left on the plant will reduce the yield. Pick them while they are small and you will realize more fruit. Growing them on the fence will help you not to miss the cucumbers as you might easily do if the vine were trailing on the ground. The leaves face the south during the summer and you might find the cucumbers hard to see if you pick from within the garden. Walk around the outside of the garden to find others hidden by the leaves. Make sure you pick them before they turn yellow, because the seeds start to harden at that stage.

### DANDELIONS

As salad lovers we have always had a fancy for fresh dandelion greens. For years we spent a considerable amount of time picking them from lawns in the area before we discovered we could grow our very own. You might ask why we would bother to grow them when we can pick them free. Well, the dandelion seeds you get in packets produce plants that are much larger, more tender, and less bitter. Give it a try and we can promise you that you'll never return to the lawn.

## HOW TO GROW

Plant the seeds 3 inches apart as soon as the ground can be worked. Thin them to 6 inches and they should be ready in about 8 weeks.

## HARVESTING

Pick the greens, leaving some so that they will replenish themselves. If you don't pull them up in the fall you'll find a healthy crop coming up the following spring.

## DILL

Don't think pickles—think salad, pot roast, zucchini, gravy, and soup, and you will realize the many uses of dill. You will find that you can benefit from the leaves as well as from the spray and seeds.

## RECOMMENDED VARIETY

Bouquet

## HOW TO GROW

Although they grow quite tall, dill plants produce next to no shade, so they will do well against the fence (for support) at the south end of the garden. We plant them in slits about 6 inches apart. Start them early in the spring so they will be ready about the time the cucumbers are the size for pickling (now think pickles).

## HARVESTING

To harvest, cut a few sprays from each plant any time you wish. Cut the heads, or sprays, before they turn dark brown, or you will lose the seeds.

## EGGPLANT

Eggplant is a real favorite around the Rockmore farm. It can be served many ways; sometimes we slice it thin and deep-fry it. Eggplant tastes so good we're convinced that someday it will be even more popular than the good old American French fry.

## RECOMMENDED VARIETIES

Dusky, Black Magic, Black Beauty, Early Long Purple, Jersey King

## HOW TO GROW

This warm-weather plant should be set in the ground a good 3 weeks after the last frost. As you do with tomatoes, keep a sharp eye out for cutworms, and to be sure of having no problems, wrap a little wax paper or foil around the stems at planting.

We stake these plants because they are very heavy and a strong wind can do a lot of damage.

Try to grow only 6 fruits per plant by pinching off blossoms.

### HARVESTING

Pick the fruit when they are dark purple and glossy. If they lose their sheen, remove them (good for composting) to encourage formation of new fruit. Don't wait until the fruit has reached its maximum size before picking and always use a knife or shears to harvest because the stems of most eggplants are quite prickly and tough.

### ENDIVE

Endive is a delicious vegetable that everyone should provide room for in the garden. It's easy to grow and needn't be bitter in taste. It can be cooked as well as used in salads.

### RECOMMENDED VARIETIES

Green Curled, Florida Deep Heart, Broad Leaved, Batavian

### HOW TO GROW

We do not suggest spring planting of endive because it invariably becomes bitter as the days become warmer. Try planting during the midsummer, after some departed spring crops have left room in the Carpet Garden. If you do it this way, we can guarantee the fall flavor will be less bitter.

The distance apart that you plant your endive depends on whether it is large-headed or not. Be sure to check the instructions on the seed package.

### HARVESTING

One sure method of doing away with the bitter taste of endive is to tie the outer leaves with a rubber band. This is called "blanching" and should be done for approximately three weeks. Leaving the rubber bands on for a longer period may cause the heart of the plant to rot. If you choose not to blanch, pick either the full head or, like lettuce, just pick the outer leaves.

### GARLIC

Since a few cents keeps us in enough garlic to last months, we don't bother to grow it any longer. But, if you want people to keep their distance, or you are thinking about starting a roadside stand (not a bad idea nowadays), then read on.

Go to your local supermarket and buy the largest garlic bulb you can find. Make sure it is firm and contains large cloves.

### HOW TO GROW

Separate the cloves and plant them about 4 inches apart in slits at the south end of the Carpet Garden. Place the cloves about 1 inch deep if you plant in the spring. If you would like larger bulbs (and,

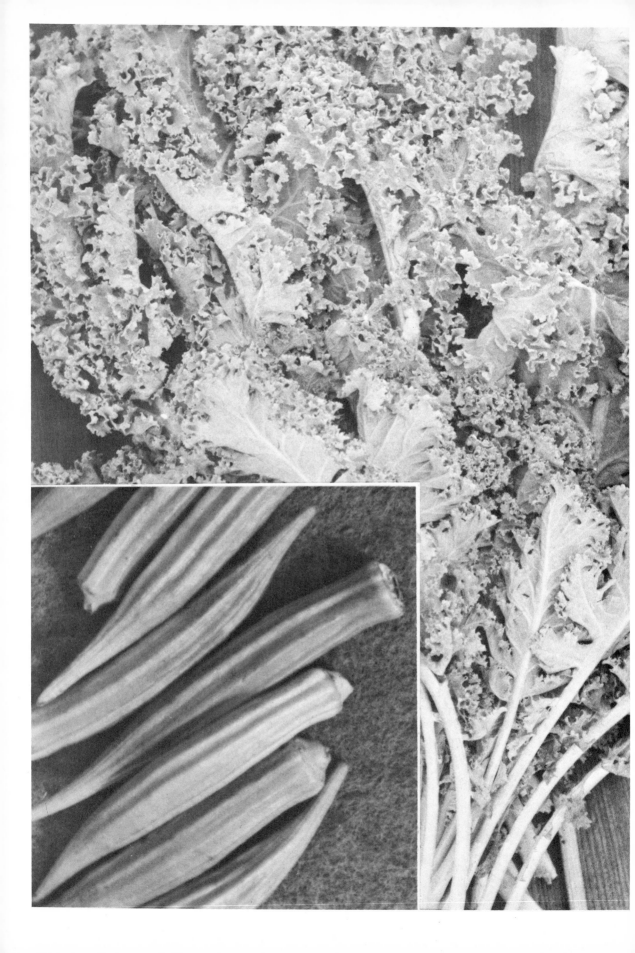

I think, better), plant them about 3 inches apart and in the middle of July. Figure on 3 months for them to mature.

### HARVESTING, STORAGE

Clip some of the green shoots while they are growing to try in salads or however you choose. When the shoots brown, or start to fall over, dig up the bulbs. Let them dry on the carpet, then bring them in. You can bag or braid them and allow to dry for a few weeks before taking them to your cellar.

## KALE

Instead of learning to love a plant that is difficult to grow, why not try kale? It is the hardiest green, can be harvested from under the snow, is great in salads and soups, and is loaded with vitamins. And, if there's a pet rabbit out back, I can promise loud applause.

### RECOMMENDED VARIETIES

Vates, Dwarf Green Scotch, Siberian, Dwarf Blue Curled Vates, Blue Curled Scotch

### HOW TO GROW

Kale is at its best when planted in mid-season (perhaps in places vacated by some spring crops) and harvested in the fall after it turns cool. Read the packets: some recommend 6-inch spacing; others as much as 20 inches. They grow to be 3 feet tall, so place them at the south end of the garden.

### HARVESTING

You will find the flavor improved after light frosts. Don't till kale under when the killer frost comes, because it will really be fine under the snow until February. Cut the outer leaves to be used in cooking (use it as you would spinach). For salads, cut the entire plant and use the tender inner leaves.

### LETTUCE

As soon as the ground can be worked, you can plant lettuce seed, for it can live through a few frosts. Why not start the seed indoors, 3 to 4 weeks before the last frost?

Then break off the outer leaves of the head lettuce varieties and plant them a few inches apart. Lettuce will bolt (go to seed) in hot weather, so plan on spring and early-fall growing seasons. Some lettuce bolts too readily, but if you try varieties that rarely bolt, you might get through the summer without having to buy lettuce from the market. Lettuce matures anytime from 40 to 95 days, so check the packet before you plant.

Bibb (bolts readily but is fine for spring planting)
Black-Seeded Simpson
Buttercrunch (slow to bolt)
Romaine (slow to bolt in cooler climates)
Salad Bowl (slow to bolt)

## *HOW TO GROW*

Plant lettuce in slits at the south end of the garden since there are few plants that it can shade. We plant most varieties 4 to 5 inches apart, and head lettuce, 6 inches. If you want large heads, the standard recommendation is 12 or more inches, but we think small heads that can be eaten in one meal are handier than large heads that end up having to be refrigerated.

Plant seeds during the last week of July for the fall crop.

## *HARVESTING*

Pick the outer leaves of all but head lettuce and the plant will continue to develop new leaves. In this way, you don't have to pull up a plant every time you want salad.

## *MELONS*

The many kinds of melons have different demands, as you can see by the seed packets or catalog. However, we shall try to generalize. Most of them seem partial to soil that is on the sandy side. This is preferred because melons do not care for too much rain and humidity. Sandy soils, of course, do not encourage the water to linger.

## *RECOMMENDED VARIETIES*

Minnesota Midget, Burpee Hybrid, Persian, Crenshaw, Kazakh

## *HOW TO GROW*

Melons can be started indoors a few weeks before the last frost. Peat pots work well because they fit right into the hole in the carpet. We use 3 seeds per 3-inch-diameter pot and set them outdoors when the soil is good and warm. Place them where they will get lots of sun, as on the north side against the fence. Carefully wrap some newspaper or wax paper around the stems to discourage cutworms. Hot caps are a good idea, to safeguard the young plants from a few cool nights.

## *HARVESTING*

The very best time to harvest a mature melon is when the stem pulls off the vine fairly easily and cleanly, leaving a smooth depression in most varieties. Toward the end of the season, pick off all the tiny melons. They won't have time to ripen and this will direct the plant's energies to the remaining larger melons.

## MUSTARD

Mustard is just loaded with vitamin A. It's great either in a salad or as a cooked green and does well in almost all climate regions.

### RECOMMENDED VARIETIES

Green Wave, Southern Giant Curled, Florida Broad Leaf, Tendergreen

### HOW TO GROW

Because mustard grows to be about knee high, a good place for it is toward the south end of the Carpet Garden. Plant as soon as the ground can be worked in the spring, and again in late summer for fall harvesting since it will bolt to seed in summer. Mustard matures 4 to 5 weeks after planting. The mustard plants are spaced from 2 to 3 inches apart, so you might think of growing a light crop between other plants, cutting additional holes in the carpet to receive them. Mustard can be planted a few inches apart in the slit cutouts at the south end of the garden but must be thinned either for additional planting or to be used as you would a mature plant.

If you are troubled by aphids, a medium spray from the garden hose will do the job.

### HARVESTING

Snap off the leaves as you need them. When leaves are from 3 to 4 inches in size, they are best in salads. Larger leaves are fine for cooking.

## OKRA

If your particular climate region is subject to hot and humid summers, you should be able to grow this fine vegetable. Okra is wonderful breaded and fried, in a soup, or in seafood gumbos, and once you've tried it, you may wonder why more home gardeners don't grow it.

### RECOMMENDED VARIETIES

Emerald, Clemson Spineless (these pods have no prickles), Dwarf Green

### HOW TO GROW

The soil temperature must reach 70 to 75 degrees in order for okra to sprout. These tall plants will throw a lot of shade so plant them at the north end of the Carpet Garden where they'll benefit from the support of the fence.

### HARVESTING

Harvest okra 4 to 5 days after the flowers open. Pods that are left on the plants will not only become tough but will sap the strength of the plant. Okra can be harvested until the first killer frost.

93

 *ONIONS*

Onions can be planted from sets or seeds. A rule of green thumb might be: from sets for large onions and from seeds for scallions. We prefer to use sets, but you can debate this over the back fence for hours. Try both ways to find which method best suits you.

Onions have few enemies and so they can be left in the garden without worry during that two-week hard-earned vacation.

### RECOMMENDED VARIETIES

Spanish Onions (From sets; sweet and cannot be stored for too long)
Southport Yellow Globe (from sets)
Red Onions (Plant from sets; both are good for storage):
   Burgundy
   Southport Red Globe
Bunching (For scallions):
   Beltsville Bunching
   Evergreen Bunching

### HOW TO GROW

If planting from seed, start onions indoors in January. When shoots grow to approximately 6 inches, trim them back to 4 inches. Keep doing this. Set them out as soon as you can (onions don't mind frosts).

Place them close together in slits at the south end of the Carpet Garden. If you want scallions or plan to use thinnings in salads, thin the plants to 1 inch apart for small onions; 3 to 4 inches if they are to be large.

Sets can also be planted early. If you want large onions, place them a good 5 inches apart. We don't recommend planting any set that is more than ¾ inches across. A set this size tends to bolt to seed.

Break off any seed pods that may start to develop at the tops of the shoots. Removing dirt from the sides of the bulbs will allow them to expand much better.

### HARVESTING

Wait until the tops start drooping naturally, then gently bend them over the rest of the tops. After most of the tops turn brown, pull the onions. If you wait too long, the bulbs will soften and even rot. (Be sure to remove any excess earth from the roots or the onions will continue to grow and will undoubtedly soften.)

Spread the onions out on the carpet to dry for about one week, making sure to turn them occasionally. Once they are dry, break off the tops and put them in mesh bags for hanging. If your onions are dried properly they should last the winter. Even Bermuda onions can last until February.

## PARSLEY

There is no reason ever to buy parsley because it is so easy to grow. Not only will you find it handy in the kitchen but you might want to give a thought toward potting it as gifts for friends. Like chives, this gift will last all winter.

### RECOMMENDED VARIETIES

Banquet
Hamburg (for roots)
Champion
Plain Italian (dark green celery-leaf type)
Moss Curled (best for salads)
Paramount

### HOW TO GROW

We recommend starting seeds inside because they take about three weeks to sprout. These short plants will do well in the south end of the garden. Four or five plants will be sufficient for any family. Harvest sparingly until late fall.

### HARVESTING

Pick the outer stems in the morning before the oils and flavor can evaporate. Use them fresh, or hang them up to dry. Parsley will live quite well through the winter in mild regions but should be transferred to pots in most areas. Trim the plants back a bit and bring them into a nice sunny spot. Keeping them pinched will help to encourage new growth.

## PEAS

The taste of fresh peas is a delight to many people, and if you are one of these and if you live in a climate that has a reasonably long cool-weather period, then it is worth your while to give peas the large garden space that they require. However, even if you don't have much room, you can try one slit of peas in your Carpet Garden.

### RECOMMENDED VARIETIES

Tall:
   Alderman, Melting Sugar
Heat resistant and about 2 feet high:
   Green Arrow, Little Marvel, Wando

### HOW TO GROW

Plant the seeds in slits about 1 inch apart. It is a good idea to purchase seeds that have been treated with a fungicide. If this is your first time growing peas, order a small package of "inoculant" from a seed catalog; this will encourage better growth by providing a special type of soil bacteria that supplies the peas with the nitrogen they need.

### HARVESTING

When the pods have become nicely rounded, begin harvesting. It is important to keep picking them every few days because mature pods if left on the plants will prevent other peas from forming. Be careful to hold on to the plant with one hand while pulling off the pods with your other hand so that you don't break the vines.

### PEPPERS

We have never had a year that our garden did not produce fine peppers. We have friends who have gardens that produce nothing but pepper flowers and no fruit. We can't figure it out, and can only suggest that they put in a Carpet Garden immediately.

Unless you own a greenhouse, we think it is a waste of time and money to grow peppers from seed. Why spend months tending them, only to put out puny plants in your garden? For little cost you can buy fine plants from a greenhouse.

### RECOMMENDED VARIETIES

Sweet or Bell:
   Lady Bell, Canape, Bell Boy, Keystone Resistant Giant
Hot Peppers:
   Hot Portugal, Cayenne, Red Chili, Hungarian Wax

### HOW TO GROW

Place the peppers in the center of the garden, about 8 to 10 inches apart. Drive in a stake at the northern edge of each hole to be used when the plant grows taller; doing this later could damage the roots.

### HARVESTING, STORAGE

Pick the bell peppers when they attain mature size and are still firm and green. You may want some red ones, but why not wait until later on in the season, for, like many vegetables, overripe fruit slows down plant production.

Wear gloves to pick hot peppers and don't touch your face with your hands—it can be quite painful. Wait at least until they are good and dry (and then be careful!). String them with stout thread and hang them. They are very pretty and can be kept strung in the kitchen.

If you like bell peppers, grow lots of them. They are a snap to freeze because they need no blanching. Just break them up into pieces and put them into strong plastic bags. You can cook with them all winter.

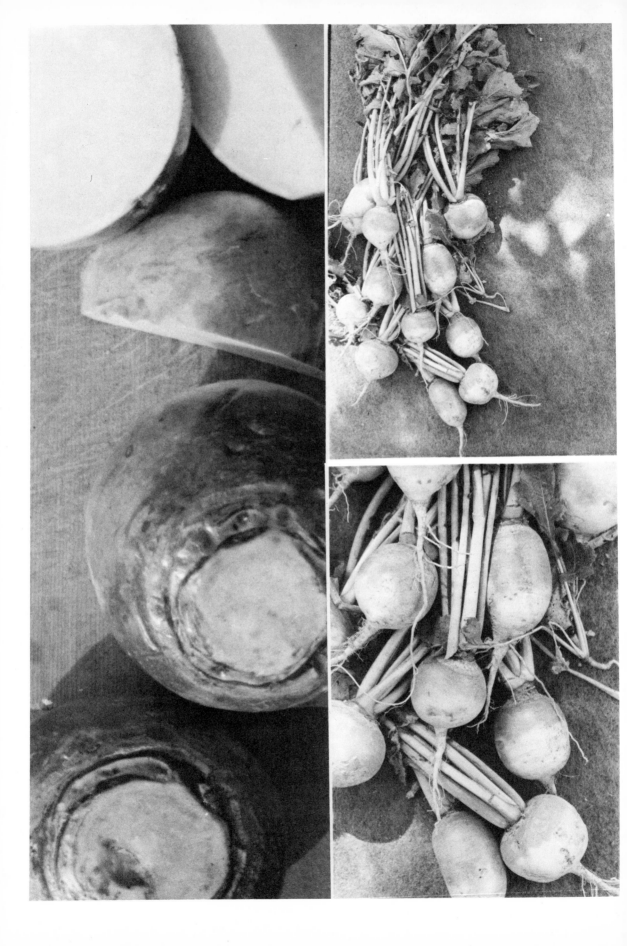

## SHALLOTS

In a pinch, onions can substitute for shallots—but only substitute. The delicate flavor of shallots is a must in fine cooking. But, like many fine things, they are so expensive! There seems to be little reason for this, because they are easy to grow. Look in gardening magazines, and you may find places to send for them. Starting plants or seeds can sometimes be found at your local greenhouse.

### HOW TO GROW

If you cannot send for them or find them in a plant store, buy as many bulbs as needed from the market (and faint at the price). Separate the cloves. Plant them at the south end of the garden, where you would onions, about 4 inches deep and as many inches apart.

### HARVESTING, STORAGE

When the tops die, pull up the shallots and dry them on the carpet as you would onions. Hang them for at least a month in a well-aired place. They can then be stored for the winter. Save a few bulbs until spring for planting. Bon appétit!

## SPINACH

Spinach, like carrots, is a crop that grows best in cool regions, so you could have some trouble raising it. There is a bit of gambling in all gardening, so why not take a chance with spinach? The summer could be a cool one, and you might well have a fine crop in an area where it is a rare event.

### RECOMMENDED VARIETIES

Spring types:
   Viking, America, Dark Green Bloomsdale
Fall types:
   Hybrid 7, Dixie Market, Hybrid 56, Virginia Savoy

### HOW TO GROW

Plant spinach as soon as the soil can be worked. Thin the plants to 5 or 6 inches apart. Read the packets carefully before you buy. Some are best for spring planting, some for fall, and there is even a blight-resistant variety that is best to plant during midsummer. To stimulate new growth, pick the outermost leaves.

### HARVESTING

When 4 to 5 leaves appear, cut the plant down below the lowest leaf. If you wait too long, it is apt to bolt to seed. When 3 to 4 new leaves appear, cut the plant back again.

 *SQUASH*

Both the winter and summer types of squash are grown pretty much the same, so we might as well put them together. Summer varieties should be planted just after the last frost and harvested during the summer months. Winter squashes should be planted in June (check the seed packet), and picked in the fall. Because they take up so much space, think about growing the bush types, or plant them to grow on, or through, the fence.

### RECOMMENDED VARIETIES
Summer squash:
  Golden Girl, Burpee Hybrid, White Bush Scallop
  (See also Zucchini, page 106.)
Winter Squash:
  Table Ace, Buttercup, Acorn, Kindred, Bush Ebony, Butternut,
  Hubbard

### HOW TO GROW
Most winter squashes need a bit more space than the summer varieties. They seem to do best in the Carpet Garden when planted in groups 16 inches apart, while summer squashes thrive when placed 10 inches apart. Plant 5 to 8 seeds per large hole and thin to the healthiest 3.

### HARVESTING, STORAGE
To prolong the harvest, pick frequently. Try using the buds, just before they open into flowers, in soups, stews, and with meats. We enjoy them best sautéed in butter and served separately.

Pick summer squash before the skin turns hard and before the squash attains a length of 10 inches. Color helps to determine when some squash is ready. With acorn squash, the skin turns dark green; butternut turns from yellow to tan; and buttercup to dark green. When storing winter squash, be sure to leave at least 2 inches of stem, or they will rot from the stem end. Remember this rule: the thicker the skin, the longer they will store. Eat the stemless and the thin-skinned first.

 *TOMATOES*

Few gardens are planted without this "king" of all vegetables (although it is technically a fruit). In most gardens, however, there is usually no more than one variety.

When planting tomatoes, we suggest trying several kinds. No variety is totally disease-resistant and anyone who thinks he will "luck out" with the first try is taking a real chance.

In selecting tomato plants for the Carpet Garden, we would suggest you visit your local nursery or greenhouse and ask the manager to prepare a container of mixed plant varieties. You'll soon discover which plants are best suited to your climate and soil.

Some gardeners, in their desire to have the first tomato in the neighborhood, plant before the last frost, protect the plants for days, and continue to grow them while the weather is still cool to cold. The end result of all this effort is usually disappointing because harsh weather can severely cut back on the crop.

Wait a little while and plant when the weather is warm. Holding off until warm days and warm earth may not get you the first tomato in the neighborhood, but it will surely get you the biggest.

Most greenhouse owners will tell you that the early planters are their favorite customers; many of them must buy a second crop after the first has died from the cold.

### RECOMMENDED VARIETIES

Harris Moreton
Red Pak
Jet Star
Supersonic
Fireball (extra early)
Big Boy
Rutgers 39 (the old standard—but much improved)
Heinz 1350 (crack-resistant)
Paste types:
   Napoli, Roma, Sunray (yellow)

### HOW TO GROW

Before planting, always pick off the bottom leaves. Plant the tomatoes deep enough so that just the top leaves are above ground. The buried stem will sprout roots and the plant will be that much stronger.

Place your tomatoes against the north fence and, as they grow, tie them every few feet with Twist-ems for support. When the plants grow to the top of the fence, pick off the tops. Now the plants can expend their energy toward fruit production rather than the production of leaf and vine.

### HARVESTING

Little needs to be told about harvesting tomatoes except to be sure that you have a salt shaker in your back pocket at all times.

### TOMATOES, CHERRY TYPE

We have chosen to list this "little king" of the garden separately from its larger cousin because many people do not have room for, or wish to grow, large tomatoes. Also, many people regard them as different, so we shall treat them as such. However, please read what is said about tomatoes (immediately preceding) because much of that information also pertains here.

### RECOMMENDED VARIETIES

Small Fry, Presto, Sweet 100, Patio (ping-pong-ball size), Red Cherry

### HOW TO GROW

If they will not be shaded by other plants, against the north fence is a good place for cherry tomatoes. They grow to about 2 feet high, at the most. If you have to put them toward the center of the garden, we think they should be staked. Follow the instructions for growing ordinary-size tomatoes.

### HARVESTING

These plants produce a lot of fruit. We feel that 2 or 3 plants will take care of the needs of most families. Pick cherry tomatoes when they are still firm, and you will find that they will refrigerate quite well.

### TURNIPS, RUTABAGAS

Turnips mature at any time from 45 to 60 days and wilt in hot weather, so plant early for an early harvest. And try a fall harvest, as well. Rutabagas need at least 90 days, so plant in mid-July and keep them in the ground until frost. Lots of people find the tastes of turnips and rutabagas too strong for them. Try mashing them with potatoes—one part turnips to three parts potatoes. We have never found anyone who didn't like them this way.

### RECOMMENDED VARIETIES

Turnips
   Tokyo Market, Golden Ball, Purple-Top White Globe, Just Right
Rutabagas
   Macomber, American Purple Top, Laurentian, Alta Sweet

### HARVESTING, STORAGE

Turnip greens are fine, cooked or raw, if you pick leaves that are smaller than your hand. Pull the turnips when they are about 2 inches in diameter. We find that they develop an unpleasant odor when stored, so you might try two harvests. But rutabagas store well. After you pull them, wash and dry the topped roots and coat them with wax. Melt paraffin in a pan and quickly dip and turn the turnip to coat evenly. You will have to peel the turnips, of course, before cooking.

 *ZUCCHINI*

Because zucchini has become so popular, and because, unlike other squashes, it is so easy to grow, we have given it a separate entry here. If you want a child's first garden to be a rousing success, encourage him to plant zucchini. Two zucchini plants are enough for any family. Any more plants, and you'll need willing neighbors or a waiting compost heap.

### RECOMMENDED VARIETIES

Rather than a list, let us say that we have not heard of a poor variety. But buy two different packets and try one plant of each kind. Don't worry, most of the seeds will keep for years.

### HOW TO GROW

Plant zucchini on the sides, outside of the carpet area, not actually in the Carpet Garden. They demand too much room. The zucchini plants' broad leaves will shade out most weeds, so little work will be required. Plant the seeds after the soil warms up. They seem to do best in hills of 2 to 3 plants, so plant 6 seeds and then thin.

What with all that fruit and such large leaves, zucchini plants get pretty thirsty, so, during the dry part of the summer, pull out the hose and give them a good drink.

### HARVESTING

Pick zucchini when they are about 8 inches long. Don't let them get much larger, and keep them picked, because this will keep the plant blossoming. You may run short of ways to prepare them for the table, but we doubt you will run short of zucchini.

# APPENDIX 1

## Mail-Order Seed Companies

W. F. Allen Company, Salisbury, Maryland 21801
Brittingham Plant Farms, Salisbury, Maryland 21801
Burgess Seed & Plant Company, Galesburg, Michigan 49053
W. Atlee Burpee Company, Philadelphia, Pennsylvania 19132
Burrell Seed Company, Rocky Ford, Colorado 81067
Conner Company, Augustus, Arkansas 72006
De Giorgi Company, Council Bluffs, Iowa 51501
Desert Seed Company, Inc., El Centro, California 92243
Evans Plant Company, Ty Ty, Georgia 31795
Farmer Seed & Nursery Company, Faribault, Minnesota 55021
Gurney Seed & Nursery Company, Yankton, South Dakota 57078
Joseph Harris Company, Inc., Rochester, New York 14624
Herbst Brothers Seedsmen, Inc., Brewster, New York 10509
Le Jardin du Gourmet, Ramsey, New Jersey 07446
J. W. Jung Seed Company, Randolph, Minnesota 53956
Keystone Seed Company, Hollister, California 95023
Kilgore Seed Company, Inc., Sanford, Florida 32771
Earl May Seed & Nursery Company, Shenandoah, Iowa 51601
L. L. Olds Seed Company, Madison, Wisconsin 53701
George W. Park Seed Company, Greenwood, South Carolina 29646
Piedmont Plants, Albany, Georgia 31702
R. H. Shumway Seedsmen, Rockford, Illinois 61101
Seedway, Inc., Hall, New York 14463
Spring Hill Nurseries, Tipp City, Ohio 45371
Stokes Seeds, Inc., Buffalo, New York 14240
Sunset Plant Farms, Chula, Georgia 31773
Otis S. Twilley, Salisbury, Maryland 21801
Vaughan's Seed Company, Downers Grove, Illinois 60515
Vista Green Farms, Vista, California 92803
Wetsel Seed Company, Harrisburg, Virginia 22801

# APPENDIX 2

## Double-Cropping Vegetables

If you care to use double cropping or planting a second crop to produce an even more profitable harvest, we have prepared the following table for you:

### PLANTING VEGETABLES ACCORDING TO GROWTH TIME

| GROUP 1 | GROUP 2 | GROUP 3 | GROUP 4 |
|---|---|---|---|
| Crops that will occupy the ground for a year or more | Crops planted early that occupy the ground only first part of season | Crops that occupy the ground the major part of the season | Crops to be planted in July and later for fall and winter gardens |
| Asparagus | Early beets | Bush and pole beans | Beets |
| Rhubarb | Early cabbage | Cabbage | Carrots |
| Chives | Lettuce | Celery | Broccoli |
| Horseradish | Onion sets | Sweet corn | Cauliflower |
| Winter onions | Peas | Cucumbers | Endive |
| Herbs | Radishes | Eggplant | Kale |
| Raspberries | Early spinach | Muskmelons | Kohlrabi |
| Strawberries | Mustard | Okra | Radishes |
| Blackberries | Turnips | Peppers | Spinach |
|  |  | Potatoes | Turnips |
|  |  | Pumpkins | Collards |
|  |  | Squash | Lettuce |
|  |  | Tomatoes |  |
|  |  | Watermelons |  |
|  |  | Swiss chard |  |

111

# APPENDIX 3

## The Carpet Gardener's Easy Planting Chart

We have assembled this easy-to-use chart to provide you with some basic and specific information regarding the planting of each individual vegetable you may wish to grow. For more detailed information about the proper spacing and arrangement of plants in the Carpet Garden, please refer to our chapter "Planting Your Carpet Garden." The age-old rule for the proper depth in the placing of seeds in the soil—about four times the length of the seed—is a good one. But if you like your measurements more exact, use our guide below. Remember that the *time* to put out the seeds and the gestation period required will differ, of course, depending on the climate of your area and its corresponding effect on the temperature of the soil. Remember also that the variety of vegetable you plant will determine, along with the climate of your area and the corresponding time at which you actually put it in the ground, the actual harvest time. So use our chart as a general guide. As we have explained to you, certain vegetables are better grown outside the Carpet Garden area. You will see that we have indicated this on the chart. However, we have included these vegetables in the chart for those of you who want to grow them anyway.

| VEGETABLE | Holes, slits, or outside the Carpet Garden area | Set out transplants | Plant seeds outdoors | Days from planting to sprouting | Depth to plant seeds | Seed to harvest (*setting out transplants) | REMARKS |
|---|---|---|---|---|---|---|---|
| Asparagus | 0 | Fall, winter early spring | | | | 2 yrs.* | Perennial, 3 yrs. from seed. Grow from plants or roots. |
| Beans | | | | | | | |
| Bush snap | H | | Mid spring–early summer | 7–14 | 1" | 50–60 days | Warm weather needed |
| Pole snap | H | | Mid spring–early summer | 7–14 | 1" | 60–70 days | Will bear produce over longer period |
| Bush lima | H | | Early–mid summer | 14–21 | 1" | 65–75 days | Long, warm summers needed |
| Pole lima | H | | Early–midsummer | 14–21 | 1" | 80–95 days | Start indoors in peat pots where summer short |
| Beets | S | | After frost to fall | 14–21 | ½" | 45–65 days | Don't like warm weather |
| Broccoli | H | After frost, late summer–fall | Early spring, midsummer | 7–14 | ½" | 50–90 days* | Strictly a cool weather plant |
| Cabbage | H | After frost, late summer | Midsummer | 7–14 | ½ | 50–80 days | Strictly a cool weather plant |
| Chinese cabbage | H | | Midsummer | 7–14 | ½ | 65–80 days | Cool weather only, do not transplant |

| VEGETABLE | Holes, slits, or outside the Carpet Garden area | Set out transplants | Plant seeds outdoors | Days from planting to sprouting | Depth to plant seeds | Seed to harvest (*setting out transplants) | REMARKS |
|---|---|---|---|---|---|---|---|
| Carrots | S | N | Early spring fall | 14–21 | ½ | 65–75 days | Keep soil loose and seedbed moist. Prefer cool weather. |
| Cauliflower | H | After frost, late summer–fall | | 14–21 | ½ | 60–100 days* | Strictly a cool weather plant |
| Celery | S | After frost, late summer | | 14–21 | ⅛ | 100–135 days* | Strictly a cool weather plant |
| Chard, Swiss | S | | Early spring, late summer | 14–21 | ½ | 45–60 days | Tolerates summer heat |
| Collards | S | | Mid–late spring, late summer–fall | 7–14 | ½ | 75–85 days | Warm weather only |
| Corn Early | O | | Early–late summer | 7–14 | 1" | 60–65 days | Plant where warm season is short |
| Mid-season | O | | Early–midsummer | 7–14 | 1" | 65–80 days | Medium-size ears |
| Late | O | | Early summer | 7–14 | 1" | 80–90 days | Usually larger plants and ears |
| Cress | S | | Early–mid-spring | 7–14 | ½" | 45 days | Hose frequently. Watercress grows 50 days to harvest. |
| Cucumbers | H | | Early–midsummer | 7–14 | 1" | 55–65 days | Warm weather only |

| Plant | Type | Start indoors | Season (outdoors) | Germination (days) | Depth | Time to harvest | Notes |
|---|---|---|---|---|---|---|---|
| Eggplant | H | Midspring–early summer | | 14–21 | ¼ " | 65–80 days* | Start indoors 8–10 weeks before last frost |
| Endive | S | | Early spring late summer | 14–21 | ¼ " | 65–90 days | Prefers cool weather |
| Garlic | S | | Early spring winter | 7–14 | 1 " | 80–90 days | Grows fast from sets (cloves) |
| Horseradish | S | Fall, late winter, early spring | | 14–28 | N | 9 mos* | Plant roots 2 " below soil surface |
| Kale | S | | Early spring late summer | 7–14 | ½ " | 60–70 days | Tolerates frosts |
| Kohlrabi | S | — | Early-late spring, late summer-fall | 7–14 | 2 " | 55–65 days | Use greens from thinning |
| Leeks | S | Early summer late summer | Mid-late spring | 14–21 | ¼ " | 80–90 days* | Dislike temperature extremes |
| Lettuce | | | | | | | |
|   Leaf | S | | Early-late spring, late summer-fall | 14–21 | ½ " | 40–45 days | Heat hardy |
|   Romaine | S | | Late summer-fall | 14–21 | ½ " | 70–85 days | Can stand some heat |
|   Head | S | After frost | Late summer-fall | 14–21 | ½ " | 80–95 days | Requires a long cool period |
| Melons | O | Mid-late spring | Early-midsummer | 14–21 | 1 " | 80–95 days | Plant in peat pots, indoors. Must have a long warm season. |
| Mustard greens | S | | Early spring, late summer-fall | 7–14 | ½ " | 35–60 days | Does best in cool weather |

| VEGETABLE | Holes, slits, or outside the Carpet Garden area | Set out transplants | Plant seeds outdoors | Days from planting to sprouting | Depth to plant seeds | Seed to harvest (*setting out transplants) | REMARKS |
|---|---|---|---|---|---|---|---|
| Okra | S | Early summer | Early–midsummer | 14–21 | 1" | 50–60 days | Seeds should be soaked before planting |
| Onions Bunching (Green Onions) | S | | Early spring, fall | 14–21 | ¼" | 60–75 days | Harvest 25–50 days from plants |
| Bulbing (Dry onions) | S | After frost | After frost | 14–21 | ¼" | 100–120 days | Harvest 50–70 days from sets |
| Parsley | S | After frost–late spring, late summer | Early–late spring | 21–28 days | ¼" | 70–90 days | Biennial. Best to soak seeds before planting. |
| Parsnips | S | | Mid–late spring, fall | 21–28 | ¼" | 100–120 days | Can stand frost |
| Peas | H | | After frost, fall | 7–14 | 1" | 60–70 days | Cool weather only |
| Peppers | H | Mid spring–early summer | | 14–21 | ⅛" | 60–80 days | Plants should be started 8–10 weeks before transplanting |
| Radishes | S | | Early spring–fall | 7–14 | ½" | 20–50 days | Fall is the time to plant winter varieties |
| Rhubarb | S | After frost | | | | 2 yrs. (1 yr. if from roots) | Perennial. Roots should be planted in early spring |
| Rutabaga | S | | Mid–late spring, late summer | 7–14 | ½" | 90 days | Does very well as a fall crop |

| Vegetable | Type | Planting time | Days to germinate | Depth | Days to harvest | Notes |
| --- | --- | --- | --- | --- | --- | --- |
| Salsify | S | Mid–late spring | 14–21 | ½" | 120–150 days | Can be stored in root cellar during winter |
| Shallots | S | Early spring, fall | 7–14 | | 150 days | Grow from sets |
| Spinach | S | After frost, late summer | 7–14 | ½" | 40–50 days | Does best in cool weather |
| Squash Summer | O | Early–midsummer | 7–14 | 1–2" | 50–60 days | For warm weather only |
| Winter | O | Early–midsummer | 7–14 | 1–2" | 80–120 days | Pick before frost |
| Tomatoes | H | Midspring–early summer | 14–21 | ¼" | 55–90 days* | There are many varieties; you should try to choose the variety for your climate. Give hybrids a try. |
| Turnips | S | Early–late spring, late summer | 7–14 | ¼" | 35–60 days | Cool weather is best for turnips |
| Zucchini | O | Early–midsummer | 7–14 | 1–2" | 50–60 days | For warm weather only |

# BIBLIOGRAPHY

Alth, Max. *How to Farm Your Backyard the Mulch-Organic Way.* New York: McGraw-Hill Book Company, 1977.

Bowers, Warner and Lucille. *Common Sense Organic Gardening.* Harrisburg, Pa.: Stackpole Books, 1974.

Cruso, Thalassa. *Making Vegetables Grow.* New York: Alfred A. Knopf, Inc., 1975.

Fox, Helen M. *Gardening for Good Eating.* New York: Collier Books, 1943 and 1973.

Hendrickson, Robert. *The Great American Tomato Book.* Garden City, N.Y.: Doubleday & Company, Inc., 1977.

Heriteau, Jacqueline. *The How to Grow and Can It Book of Vegetables, Fruits, and Herbs.* New York: Hawthorn Books, Inc., 1976.

Rice, Eddy. *How to Grow, Preserve & Store All the Food You Need.* Reston, Va.: Reston Publishing Company, Inc., 1977.

Seymour, E. L. D., ed. *The Wise Garden Encyclopedia.* New York: Grosset & Dunlap, Inc., 1970.

Tyler, Hamilton, *Gourmet Gardening.* New York: Van Nostrand Reinhold Company, 1972.

# INDEX

121